Basic Automobile Maintenance

by

Dennis Caprio

Howard W. Sams & Co., Inc.
4300 WEST 62ND ST. INDIANAPOLIS, INDIANA 46268 USA

Preface

I doubt that our creator ever intended for mankind and machinery to coexist with anything close to a peaceable relationship. Regard your automobile. It's difficult to imagine living without at least one, but on the other hand, it's frequently impossible to live with any of them. Our cars sit safely nestled in garages and on driveways or rest uncomfortably on city streets, exposed to the whims of the careless, all the while waiting to hustle us to the local market or across the country. Like dogs, they can be mankind's best friends.

And like dogs, no matter how often or how much you would like to forget about them, they need attention. Left to their own devices, cars grow discontented, cantankerous, and every so often decide to stop working just when you need them the most. The inconvenience is frustrating, and the repairs are often expensive.

The care and feeding of your car is what this book is all about. Think of it as you might think of a book that discusses steps for you to take to prevent yourself from coming down with a cold. It's a book of automobile preventive medicine that you can administer yourself, and it's a book of simple cures that you can work in your own garage. You don't have to be a machinery medicine man; you merely have to read carefully, think, and care a little for the whirring, clanking, and sliding parts that make your car what it is.

You might discover that caring for your car is entertaining or boring or frustrating or what-have-you, but one thing it always is . . . it is CHEAPER. Clean out your garage; set up your tool box; puff up your confidence and patience; and enjoy yourself.

Dennis Caprio

Acknowledgments

My thanks to Richard Korn who performed admirably before my camera; to Firestone Tire and Rubber Company who sent photos on extremely short notice; and to Jim Clark and the Lexington Senior High School who opened their auto shop doors and allowed me to photograph some of their teaching aides.

Contents

CHAPTER 1

Life With Your Car

Nearly everyone who owns a car would like to drive it, trouble free, for the duration that it is in his or her possession. Some of us consider it an inalienable right, while others merely wish it were so. Remarkably enough, millions of us have been fortunate and able to do just that, whereas thousands of others wail with angry frustration about their infamous lemons.

Fortune does play a minor role in the dependability and longevity of any motor vehicle. The machines are made by men and women who control other machines, and however carefully guarded, mistakes are inevitable. That is why manufacturers offer warranties and toll-free telephone numbers that are connected to their customer relations offices.

Generally speaking, the recommended doses of thoughtful care and maintenance will keep your car running well and looking good for thousands and thousands of miles. A great many modern drivers, however, regard their cars as mere appliances, like a toaster or coffee pot, that they can take for granted. These people have little or no respect for, interest in, or understanding of the parts that go round-and-round and up-and-down. In many cases, they are the first owners to shout "LEMON" when something breaks and the first to accuse the manufacturer of shoddy workmanship.

You have a number of car care alternatives available to you, the most logical of which is the manufacturer's franchised dealer. The dealer is a sales and service representative of the parent company. Usually, his service department is stocked with the best and latest information, the finest special tools and testing equipment, and the cream of the factory-trained mechanics. Ideally, the dealer's service department acts as a kind of assembly line extension where predelivery service checks up on the maker's quality control, and where after-sales problems are solved and general maintenance is performed. But all too often, reality is far from ideal.

I think all of us can agree that, on the average, dealers aren't as reliable as they once were. Most of us have heard, or can relate, grim tales about poor dealer service, but for every inept and unscrupulous one, you find five fair ones and five good ones. The reasons behind the dealers' failure to live up to our standards of customer service are complex and involve a variety of social and economic phenomena that are beyond our ability to change and perhaps understand. There is one thing with which you can effectively deal.

Sheer sales and service volume is, in large part, responsible for unsatisfactory service. Dealers are trapped in a highly competitive buyer's market where profit margins on new cars are low, and after-sales service volume is large and demanding. The dealer's effort to please all of his customers all of the time has become self-defeating. As a result, predelivery service has deteriorated into a decent clean-up and a road test to see that everything is working correctly. After-sales service has degenerated into the kind of situation where getting the car done on time takes priority over doing it correctly.

Believe it or not, most dealers try very hard to satisfy their customers' demands. Keep that thought in mind when you pick your car up from the service department. If you discover that all of the work hasn't been done or hasn't been done to your standards, take the car back. Remove the chip from your shoulder before you confront the service manager. Be firm and patient in your demands, and don't be afraid to keep taking the car back until you are satisfied. Generally, one return trip will be enough. Just remember that a little patience and understanding on both sides of the counter will go a long way toward establishing better customer/dealer relationships.

While your car is protected by the manufacturer's warranty, you are more or less stuck with a franchised dealer. Once the warranty expires, you are free to service the car yourself or to choose one of the increasingly popular independent service shops. Some are branches of large accessory companies such as Sears and Goodyear. Others specialize in chassis and exhaust work, and still others are run by factory-trained mechanics who have left dealers to start their own businesses. The quality of service may or may not be better than a dealer's, but the independents tend to be less expensive. Servicing the car yourself is one sure way of knowing exactly what you are getting.

Regardless of how carefully we treat our cars, they are still subjected to an enormous amount of abuse. Emission controls, which are absolutely necessary, create lean fuel/air mixtures in the engine's combustion chambers. As a result, cylinder head temperatures are extremely high. The increased operating temperatures tax the cooling system and make life miserable for the valves and pistons.

The higher operating temperatures place an unusual burden on the engine oil as well. In most cases, an ordinary family sedan driven in normal, everyday traffic is harder on oil than is a racing car. Oil companies responded to the needs of modern engines with additional ingredients which help slow the inevitable breakdown of the lubricating properties of oil. Filter manufacturers developed more efficient filters.

During the early seventies when this country suffered its first real shortage of crude oil since World War II, we began seeing inflation rise at a rate that we had only read about before. Auto makers discovered that folks just weren't buying new cars, and they hoped to counter the trend by making each model more economical to own. They took advantage of the oil and filter technology and extended time intervals between oil changes. Their recommendations were and are based on the ideal side of normal driving conditions and should be regarded as a base line from which to judge what is best for your car and driving habits.

Probably the worst condition is infrequent short trips during the winter months when it is cold, and the engine doesn't reach its full operating temperature. The acids and moisture that combustion produce settle in the oil and do not have a chance to evaporate. Filters can't remove these contaminants and if allowed to accumulate and sit, they eat away at the bearing surfaces. More is explained about oils, filters, and change intervals in Chapter 8.

Regardless of the weather conditions, long periods of inactivity followed by short drives do your engine little good. The protective oil film on moving parts is at its thinnest and weakest after the engine has been sitting for a long time. For the first few seconds after you start your engine, it is virtually unlubricated.

Winter in cold climates punishes body and chassis parts. Salt, sand, and cinders used to treat ice- and snow-covered highways abrade and corrode body, chassis, and exhaust parts. Frost heaves and pot holes play havoc with your car's tires, shock absorbers, springs, control arms, bushings, and linkages. Consider the chassis when you wash your car. Have the exhaust system examined for leaks and rust-weakened components at least once a year. A leaking exhaust reduces the engine's efficiency, increases fuel consumption, and might fill the passenger compartment with carbon monoxide. Slow down for frost heaves and pot holes and avoid them whenever possible. Your chassis will last longer and demand fewer adjustments.

Periodic maintenance either according to the maker's suggestions or more frequently than suggested is the best car life insurance that you can buy. Your automobile is incredibly complex yet remarkably dependable. Simple service is always less expensive than the repairs that result from neglect. Tune-ups, which you will learn how to do later in the book, let your engine run better on less gasoline for a greater number of years. Properly inflated tires, correctly adjusted suspension, and healthy components provide a safe and economical chassis.

Although manufacturers have extended time intervals between service, you shouldn't simply forget about your car's needs. Change the oil and filter frequently. Change the air cleaner and fuel filters regularly. Have wheel alignment, tires, and suspension components checked by a competent shop once a year under normal conditions, and twice a year if you drive mostly on poorly surfaced roads. Examine alternator and other belts once or twice a year, and replace them when they show signs of wear.

If you plan to tow a trailer, make sure that your brakes, suspension, and cooling systems are up to the extra load. If you respect your car, care for it at least according to the maker's suggestions, and never take any of the machinery for granted, you should be able to drive any modern domestic car for thousands and thousands of trouble-free miles.

CHAPTER 2

Diagnosis, Repair Sense, Tools, and Safety

If you have ever had a chance to watch truly fine mechanics diagnose and repair an ailing car, you might also have noticed how easy they make the job appear. The best mechanics work with a graceful fluid economy. They waste little motion and almost no time. Training and experience are, in large part, responsible for the deception, but good mechanics enjoy a natural instinct or feel for the machinery that probably can't be taught.

They know instinctively just how much torque to apply when they tighten a bolt. Many of them can sight-gap ignition points and spark plugs to within a hair of the correct feeler gauge measurement. The sound and feel of a car communicates information to them that we ordinary folks fail to recognize, and their experience translates the feedback into symptoms and cures. Many of the best mechanics like cars; some are indifferent. But all of the good ones care about the quality of the work they do.

Care is the ingredient that makes a good home mechanic and if it is coupled with enthusiasm, can make an excellent one. You will probably never be able to make the work look easy or be able to work as quickly as a professional, but you might be able to produce results as good and as satisfying as the fellow down the street who charges 15 to 20 dollars an hour for his work.

DIAGNOSIS

Unless something breaks that drastically alters your car's performance, its condition deteriorates gradually, almost imperceptibly. As you drive your car day in and day out, ignition points wear and change the timing; spark plugs wear and fire less efficiently; the air cleaner gets dirty and changes the fuel/air mixture available to the combustion chambers; shock absorbers wear, springs weaken and change the ride and handling characteristics. Constant pounding knocks the front wheels out of alignment. Tires may leak air and become too soft. Rolling resistance increases, the tread wears unevenly, and the tire carcass runs hotter than it should.

All of these things happen over a period of time, and unless you are attuned to the messages your car transmits or check it periodically, you will find yourself confronted with expensive repairs in place of simple maintenance. Unfortunately, most modern domestic cars isolate the driver from the vehicle. Soft, plush seats, thick sound insulation, power steering, power brakes, rubber dampers, and rubber bushings have made modern cars so smooth and quiet that anything short of a major failure remains undetected.

Recognizing and understanding your car's messages regarding its generally deteriorating performance and diagnosing its ills requires some practice plus a standard for comparison. If you are about to buy a new car or have just bought one, you are in luck. Generally speaking, new cars provide an excellent standard for comparison. They will be in good tune, and the chassis will be taut and responsive. Make sure that the tires are inflated to the maker's recommendation for normal driving and loads, then drive the car over a variety of roads in a variety of traffic situations. Listen to it idle, accelerate, and cruise at steady speed. Feel the engine's response. Feel the car respond to bumps and holes, cornering forces, normal and hard braking. If you have an older car, you might want to take it to a competent professional for a thorough service and use the results for future comparison.

Once you have become familiar with your car's performance characteristics when it is in top condition, you should be able to recognize the changes that wear and tear inflict upon it. Does the car stumble and hesitate when you want to accelerate? Does it take longer to reach highway speeds when you accelerate onto an interstate? Does it feel mushy and wallowy in corners or during quick lane changes? Does it stop in a straight line under normal and emergency braking? Do the brakes make noises that you've never heard before? After negotiating a dip in the road, does the car pitch up and down for some time before it settles to an even and smooth ride? Does the wind or do road irregularities make the car yaw from side to side? All of these symptoms indicate to the aware driver that his or her car needs attention and now. Open your ears and eyes. Let your car talk to you through your hands and the seat of your pants. Later on in the book, you will learn what the sights and sounds of your car mean, and you will learn how to translate the information into action.

REPAIR SENSE

Machines are a result of scientific research and development, and are, therefore, logical. Some of the things that go wrong with them may not always seem logical, but when you think about them, you will see that the causes and effects tie together as nicely as you please. Just as cause and effect are related, so are the steps that you have to take in order to make repairs.

First of all, THINK. The thousands of parts that go into making your car work in concert to produce total performance are related to one another in function, and they are related to one another in the assembly process. It stands to reason then, that if the car was assembled in a logical progression, it will come apart in the same fashion.

If, for example, you want to expose one of the front brakes, you have to remove the hubcap (the part last installed on the wheel), the wheel lug nuts, the wheel, the spindle nut cover, the spindle nut, and finally the brake drum. The same logic applies to any section of the car. Before you leap into a repair or a general maintenance procedure, examine the area, read the instructions, then proceed with the work. Refer to the instructions as often as necessary so that you can avoid mistakes.

Studying the situation before you start allows you to determine to a great extent which tools you will need for the job. The first couple of times that you tackle a job, you are bound to leave out some of the tools, but experience will soon remedy that. Until you do learn your tools, you might find it less frustrating and less time consuming to place your tool box close at hand before you get started. Substituting a tool that is convenient for the correct one that is in the box at the other end of the garage is self-defeating.

TOOLS

I can't begin to stress enough the importance of having good tools neatly arranged in a good sized tool box that is large enough for quick reference and future expansion. There's nothing quite so aggravating as having to search through a crowded, disorganized tool box for the correct wrench. It will waste time and will drive you crazy. Fig. 2-1 illustrates the complete home mechanic's tool box. It is clean, well organized, and large enough to expand your tool collection if you discover that working on cars develops into a hobby such as restoring classic and antique cars. If you

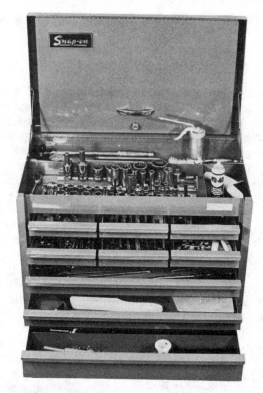

Fig. 2-1. A complete home mechanic's toolbox.

think that this setup is more than you will ever need, choose a smaller more portable box. Most tool salesmen will be able to help you with a selection. Some home mechanics have clean, neat, large garages and might want to hang tools from peg board or store them in drawers built into a workbench. Choose the setup that feels most comfortable to you and best suits your needs.

What brand tools should you buy? Probably the three best are S-K Wayne, Snap-On, and Sears Craftsman. There are, of course, many other manufacturers who make perfectly satisfactory tools that sell for less. Before you invest in a set of tools, you might want to consider how long you will keep them and how frequently you plan to use them.

Most tools are a lifetime investment, and many makers offer a lifetime guarantee on their hand tools. Although you might find equal quality among brands, you will not find equal feel. Some wrenches and screwdrivers can feel awkward in your hand or have handle shapes that hurt your hand when you apply torque to a bolt or screw. Generally, smooth, flat wrench shanks feel the most comfortable. I have found that the new triangular shaped screwdrivers provide the most power and comfort.

Wrenches

Long handled open end, box end, or combination wrenches will serve your purposes better than the short handled ones. They provide more leverage and keep your hands clear of obstructions. On the other hand, there are times when a long wrench won't fit into the work space available. Experience with your particular car will determine your choice.

Which style wrench should you choose? I prefer combination wrenches (open end on one side, box end on the other), because they offer the most versatility. The box end grips the bolt hex more securely, and open end lets you work in tight spots where the box end won't fit around the bolt. You can buy the wrenches with either six or twelve point boxes. The six point box has six flats and is best for loosening very tight nuts and bolts. The twelve point box looks like heavy inside knurling and is easier to place over the bolt where the loosening and tightening arc is limited. Generally, mechanics prefer the six point box for larger sizes (⅝ to one inch) and the twelve point box for smaller sizes (⁵⁄₁₆ to ½ inch). Sizes below ⁵⁄₁₆ come only with six point boxes. Your wrenches should range in ¹⁄₁₆ inch increments from ¼ to ¾ inch.

Whether we like it or not, the U.S. will adopt the metric measurement system. In 1974, Ford produced the first American built, all metric engine for use in the Pinto. Ford listed the engine's displacement as 2.3 liters or 2300 cubic centimeters. Even before they introduced the American built metric engine, they used a 2000cc four cylinder engine from their German works in both the Pinto and the Capri. Subsequently, Chevrolet introduced the all metric Chevette. As American auto manufacturers tool up for all new cars, they are converting to the metric system.

If your car is part metric and part SAE, like the Pinto where only the engine is metric, a small selection of metric sizes will do. The most widely used sizes include 10 millimeter (mm) 12 mm, 13 mm, 14 mm, 17 mm, and 19 mm. You might find a few 6 mm hex head bolts, and sometimes the distributor hardware will be 5½ mm or ⁷⁄₃₂ inch. If your car is all metric, the sizes listed above are still the most common, but in order to be safe you might want to fill out the selection with a 4 mm, 11 mm, 15 mm, 16 mm, 18 mm, and 22 mm. You will need equivalent sizes in your socket set.

The box end ratchet is one of the most useful wrenches available (Fig. 2-2). It can save time and effort in difficult places where positioning and repositioning a normal box or open end wrench is nearly impossible and where a ratchet and socket combination is impossible. You can buy them with two sizes to a single wrench such as a 7/16 inch at one end and a ½ inch on the other (12 mm and 13 mm in metric tools). They are available in six and twelve point. The orientation of the wrench as you place it over the bolt determines tighten (ON) or loosen (OFF). The words are stamped into the wrench shank. Two wrenches containing a total of four of the most popular sizes is a good choice.

Socket Sets

You can live without a good ratchet and socket set, but your work will be much easier if you have one. They are available in a variety of square drive sizes, the most common of which are ¼, ⅜, and ½ inch. The size of the shaft onto which the socket fits determines the drive size of the ratchet. An 8-inch, ⅜-inch drive ratchet is plenty large enough for the work discussed in this book.

Fig. 2-2. Box end ratchet.

Some ratchet gear teeth are more closely spaced than others. Make sure that the ratchet you choose allows you to engage the ratchet gear in a fairly short arc. Sockets are available in either six or twelve points. Your selection of sockets should include a special spark plug socket and a variety of other sockets in 1/16-inch increments from 5/16 to ¾ inch, or in one-millimeter increments from 10 mm to 19 mm, or perhaps 22 mm. You should include a 6- and a 12-inch extension, and one universal joint to be used for hard to get at nuts and bolts.

Miniature Socket and Wrench Sets

For small and delicate jobs, you might want to consider buying a ¼-inch drive socket/ratchet set, and an ignition wrench set. Sizes range from 7/32 inch (4 mm in metric) to 7/16 inch (to 12 mm in metric). They are easy to work with in confined spaces, and the size and length of the ratchet and wrenches limits the amount of torque that you can safely apply to the more fragile small hardware.

Screwdrivers

It seems as though a person can never have a large enough selection of screwdrivers. They range in size from the tiny to the gigantic and in shaft length from stubby to extra long. Enthusiastic professionals can spend a fortune on screwdrivers of all sorts and are able to find a use or an excuse for every one of them. For your purposes at home, a 3-inch #1 Phillips, a 4-inch #2 Phillips, an 8-inch #2 Phillips, and an 8-inch #3 Phillips will do nicely. Flat bladed screwdrivers should include a 6-inch ⅛-inch blade, a 6-inch ¼-inch blade, and an 8-inch ³⁄₁₆-inch blade. A stubby #2 Phillips and a stubby ⅛-inch flat blade will come in handy as well.

Pliers and Wire Cutters

You can buy pliers in all manner of shapes and sizes for all kinds of jobs. There are slip-joint pliers, needle-nose pliers, lineman's pliers, and channel lock or water pump pliers. As with any tool, all pliers are not created equal. The least expensive pliers have poorly matching jaws and sloppy joints, and are virtually useless for any but the most mundane jobs. If you plan to use pliers, get the best. They are easier to use, will serve you longer, and prevent the raging frustration associated with using poor quality tools. You should probably have one pair of 6-inch needle-nose, 8-inch needle-nose, 8-inch slip-joint, and a 10-inch channel lock pliers.

Although some pliers have wire cutters built into the jaws close to the pivot joint, you will be happier in the long haul with a good pair of 8-inch diagonal cutters. Once again, good quality "dikes" are a much better investment than the less expensive ones. Dikes should be made from reasonably hard steel for long wear, the cutting edges must be sharp and must meet accurately with no gaps from tip to joint.

Close the jaws, squeeze the handles together with a little pressure, and hold the jaws up to the light. You shouldn't be able to see any light at all or, at most, a barely discernible line of light along the cutting edges. An easily discernible gap means low quality dikes. Diagonal cutters are handy for cutting wire in tight spots, because the cutting surface extends all the way out to the tip of the jaws.

Miscellaneous Tools and Heavy Equipment

After you have decided upon or collected your basic tool supply, you should consider some of the odd tools that either come in handy or are essential to specific jobs. This category includes the following:

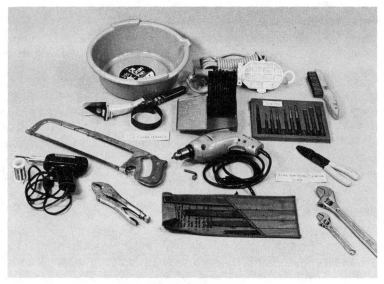

Fig. 2-3. Additional tools.

1. Hacksaw. (See Fig. 2-3 for tools from 1-14.)
2. ⅜-inch electric drill and bit set.
3. Oil filter wrench.
4. Oil can spout.
5. Drain pan.
6. Drop light.
7. Drifts.
8. Chisels.
9. Wire brush.
10. A 6-inch and a 10-inch crescent or adjustable wrench.
11. 10-inch vise-grip pliers.
12. Wire stripping and crimping tool.
13. Soldering gun.
14. Files.
15. Torque wrench. A torque wrench measures in either inch-pounds or foot-pounds the amount of twisting force that you apply to a bolt or nut. Although you will rarely need one for the basic work discussed in this book, car makers do recommend using them for torquing spindle nuts and disc brake caliper mounting bolts. For wheel bearing work, you will need a torque wrench that reads to 150 inch-pounds, and another that reads to 100 foot-pounds. See Chapter 4 for wheel bearing details.
16. Tire pressure gauge. One will do, but two, one in your tool box and one in the glove compartment, will serve you

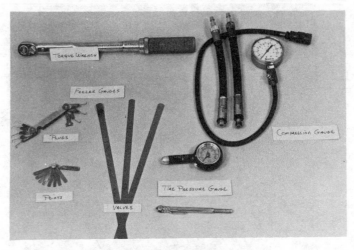

Fig. 2-4. Measuring devices.

better. The inexpensive slide gauges are good enough. If you have a thing for accuracy, buy one of the good quality dial gauges like the one shown in Fig. 2-4.

17. Compression gauge. Sometimes expensive and generally not necessary, compression gauges can help you diagnose a rough running engine. See Chapter 10 for details regarding the use of a compression gauge.

18. Valve clearance feeler gauges. The long ones shown in Fig. 2-4 are the easiest to use. Buy sizes that correspond to the manufacturer's cold valve clearance for your engine and perhaps one or two sizes over and under.

19. Allen wrench set.

20. Large breaker bar.

21. Hydraulic floor jack. (See Fig. 2-5 for hydraulic floor jack and jack stands.) As far as I'm concerned, bumper jacks are useless for anything more than emergency tire changes on the road. When you are working at home, use your hydraulic jack. It is much safer, and easier to use.

22. Jack stands. These are absolutely essential if you plan to work under the car or if you plan to rotate your car's tires at home. In the interest of safety, buy jack stands that are stronger than you think you'll need. In Chapter 4, you will learn how to place these under the car.

TESTING DEVICES

For engine tune-ups and any electrical troubleshooting work, you will need a volt-ohm-milliampere meter, a timing light, and

Fig. 2-5. Hydraulic floor jack and jack stands.

a dwell meter (Fig. 2-6). Individually, they are probably the most expensive tools in your box. Medium priced, medium quality instruments are good enough for occasional home use. You will need one hydrometer for testing the specific gravity of your battery and one for testing the cooling system antifreeze.

WORK HABITS

You don't have to be a professional mechanic to develop professional work habits. Good work habits save time and lessen the frustration that even professionals sometimes feel. Before you start a job, make sure that the work area is clean and uncluttered. Next, arrange work lights so that you can reach them easily or won't have to move them more than is necessary. Lay out the tools that you think you will need. Read the instructions through once, then refer to them as often as you need to during the job.

Because you don't have years of experience upon which to draw, work slowly and carefully. As you remove parts from the car, lay them out in order, label them if you have to, or draw a diagram of the disassembly sequence. In order to eliminate mistakes that lapses in memory cause, it's best to begin and complete a job in one session. If you begin to feel frustrated or angry, take a break and think through the procedure before you continue. Anger often upsets a person's reason and prevents him or her from thinking clearly. An angry mechanic is more likely to make mistakes than a mechanic who is completely relaxed and sure of himself.

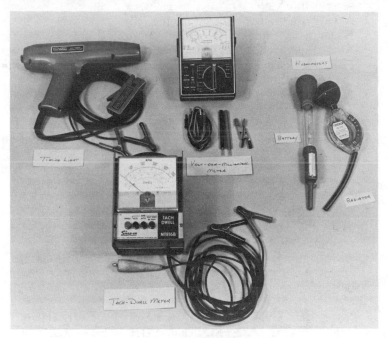

Fig. 2-6. Testing equipment.

If you have to abandon a job for several hours or overnight, make notes regarding what you have done and what remains to be done. Time away from the job may leave blank spaces in the inexperienced mechanic's mind where the next step should have been stored. You wouldn't want to leave the cotter pin out of the front wheel spindle nut and lose a wheel.

As you reassemble the car, clean and lubricate those parts that need it. Clean your tools after every job, put them back in their usual places, then clean up the entire work area. Clean-up is as much a part of a good mechanic's day as is the more challenging work, and it leaves the area and your tools ready for the next job.

SAFETY

Slow, relaxed, and careful work is essential to your safety as well as your efficiency and pleasure. A list of safety precautions follows.

1. Wipe grease and oil from your hands frequently as you work. An oil covered hand cannot grip a tool as well as a clean one, and a slip at the wrong time might result in a serious injury.
2. Always use the correct tool for the job.
3. Never work under a car that is supported only by a jack. Always use jack stands.
4. Place blocks in front of and behind both wheels opposite the end of the car that you want to jack up.
5. Avoid wearing loose, floppy clothing. Roll up your sleeves. Tie back long hair.
6. When you are observing or adjusting a component of a running engine, avoid contact with the cooling fan and all belts.
7. Place blocks in front of and behind at least one wheel and set the emergency brake when you are making adjustments on a running engine.
8. Wear safety glasses when you are working on your back under the car or when you are using an electric drill, hammer and chisel, or hammer and drift punch.
9. Never smoke while you are working on your car. Gasoline and its fumes and the vapors rising from the car's storage battery present real danger of fire or explosion.

Remember, while you are working on your car, THINK, WORK SLOWLY, AND PROCEED WITH THE SAME LOGIC THAT WENT INTO THE DESIGN AND CONSTRUCTION OF YOUR CAR.

CHAPTER 3

Exterior and Interior Care

Everyone knows that a clean and shiny car runs better than a dirty one. That statement really isn't true, but it does seem to be so doesn't it? The pride we Americans take in our cars is probably responsible for that feeling, but there's more to this clean-car business than pride. Clean, waxed body panels look better longer, and they are able to resist the cancerous rust that reduces perfectly good running cars to worthless junk. A clean interior of a car like a clean house makes time spent within more pleasant.

Maintaining the cosmetic quality of your car is more time consuming than difficult, and it requires a different sort of discipline than that which drags you into the garage for a tune-up. Because your car's appearance really doesn't affect its performance, it's easy to let it slip into almost irretrievably bad condition.

Economically speaking, cleaning and waxing returns more value per time and money spent than many other kinds of maintenance. Dealers and private sale customers will almost always pay more for a beautiful car that is suffering from a few running problems than they will pay for a car that is mechanically perfect but is rusted, dented, and has torn upholstery. That rule of thumb applies to most minor but easily discernible mechanical ills, but does not apply to cars that need major engine, transmission, differential, or suspension work.

WASHING YOUR CAR

There are no truly wrong ways to wash your car, but some are more right than others. Any kind of wash is better than none especially if you drive on salt treated roads in winter or live on an immediate coast where sea breezes blast your car with salt-laden air.

Exactly how you wash your car depends upon the condition of the painted surface. Generally, recently waxed or newly waxed cars will clean up with cold clear water and a soft sponge. You should be able to remove all but the most tenacious bugs, bird droppings, and tree sap spots from a waxed car with clear water. Also, if you wash your car once a week or so and don't allow massive amounts of road grime to build up on the body panels, washing it in clear cold water will do the trick.

On the other hand, a car which hasn't been waxed in a year or more, a car the painted surface of which is dull from the effects of air pollution and hot sun, or a car which hasn't been washed and is covered with heavy road grime or winter salt needs washing with cool or tepid water and a mild car washing soap. Never use harsh detergents or abrasive cleansers on your car.

In either case, pull your car into the shade and let the body panels cool before you wash it. Washing in the hot sun isn't good for the paint, and it makes drying to a spot-free finish nearly impossible. In winter, pull your car into a heated garage and let the body warm up before you begin washing. Water will freeze almost instantly when it contacts extremely cold sheet metal.

First, rinse the entire car with cold water under low pressure. You can use an ordinary garden hose without the high pressure nozzle. Rinsing the car before you wash it removes some of loose dust and dirt and softens what remains. Soak your sponge or terry cloth rag in a bucket of cold clear water and begin washing the roof. Use light pressure and a circular motion. Resoak the sponge frequently. Rinse the roof immediately after washing, then proceed to the hood, trunk, and sides of the car. Wash one section at a time and always rinse that section before you continue with another. Dry the surface with a clean, damp chamois or a cotton terry cloth towel. Never use a cloth made from synthetic fabric to dry your car. Synthetic fabrics don't absorb water very well, and some of them will scratch the surface.

If you car is filthy with heavy deposits of road grime or salt, rinse it first with cold water under increased pressure. Mix a car washing soap according to the maker's recommended proportions in a bucket of cool water. Soak your sponge and begin washing the roof. Use a modest amount of pressure and a circular motion. Avoid scrubbing heavily soiled areas. Grit will collect in the sponge and scratch the paint. Go over the heavily soiled areas a couple of times and rinse the sponge out each time in a separate bucket of clear water to remove the grit. Wash in sections, rinse, and dry immediately.

Vinyl Tops

Vinyl tops are good looking and popular, but they are especially susceptible to damage from air pollution and sunlight. Wash your vinyl top with a mild soap and a soft bristle brush or use a vinyl cleaner. If the top has grown dull over the years, you can restore its original shine with a preservative/restorer, available at auto supply stores.

Bugs, Birds, Sap, and Tar

Squashed bugs, bird droppings, tree sap, and road tar are a troublesome lot especially if you haven't waxed your car in some time or allow the sun to bake them onto a newly waxed surface. If you catch the organic stuff early, you can whisk it off of a freshly waxed surface with cold, clear water and a sponge. Allowed to sit, they grip the waxed surface like ticks on your dog, and they will leave stains that cannot be removed without a cleaner wax.

Bugs, bird droppings, and sap cling to an unwaxed surface more tenaciously than they do to a waxed one. Remove the heavy deposits by washing with car washing soap, remove the stains with cleaner wax, then wax the car. You can remove road tar from a freshly waxed surface with a cleaner wax and a little elbow grease. Use a good road tar cleaner on an unwaxed surface and on a heavily coated waxed surface. Always wax the car after using road tar cleaner. Never use kerosene or gasoline to remove tar from the painted surface of your car. Both chemicals are quite harsh and will damage the paint.

Chrome

Chrome is very durable, and you can keep it in top condition with the same wax that you use on the painted surfaces. Neglected chrome will rust in time, but if you catch it before it pits, a good chrome cleaner will restore the chrome to its original brilliance. There is no wax in chrome cleaner. It is made from fairly harsh chemicals that should be kept away from the paint. After cleaning the chrome, apply a healthy coat of wax.

Wheels

If your car's wheels are covered by full-size chrome discs, you will probably want to treat them as carefully as you would other chrome parts. Use chrome cleaner carefully on wheel discs that have painted inserts. Chrome cleaner will remove the paint. Uncovered wheels that have a lot of nooks and crannies will clean up nicely with car wash soap and a soft bristled wheel brush (Fig. 3-1). You can clean both black and white wall tires

Fig. 3-1. Wheel brush.

with a whitewall cleaner and your wheel brush. If you like shiny black wall tires, treat them with a rubber preservative.

Rubber Moldings, Seals, Etc.

Time and air pollution are rubber's worst enemies. Both work to make the rubber hard and brittle, a condition which makes it ugly and reduces its sealing or cushioning properties. You can keep rubber parts looking good and pliable by treating them with silicone spray or a rubber preservative.

Undercarriage

Don't forget the undercarriage when you wash your car. You can't see it, but it's there and it deserves some attention. Road grime, mud, and salt collect in hard-to-get-at spaces where they build up, hold moisture, and eat away at the undercoating and uncoated metal parts. Rinse the inside of the fenders and as much of the chassis as you can with cool water under high pressure. Coin operated car washes are ideal for this sort of cleaning.

Windows

After you have washed and dried your car, wash the windows. Any one of the popular household cleansers, or ammonia (clear) mixed 1 to 4 with water, will work just great on your car windows. Old-fashioned, 100% cotton muslin normally used to make bed sheets is the best window wiping material ever made. It's very absorbent and virtually lint-free. Synthetics or cotton/polyester blends just don't absorb water very well. Loosely wadded up newspaper works very well for wiping moisture from the windows. Terry cloth and soft paper towels work well but leave lint.

Don't neglect the inside of your windows. If you smoke cigarettes or a pipe, you'll find that the windows film over very quickly. Smoke film scatters the light from the headlights of approaching cars and sunlight in such a way that visibility is reduced to a dangerously low level. Also, clean windows are less prone to moisture fogging than are dirty ones.

Generally speaking, when the windshield wipers leave streaks of water on the glass instead of wiping them clean, it's time for a new set of blades. That rule, however, does not always apply. Many times the deposits left on your windshield contain dirt that is not water soluble. Sometimes the stuff is even resistant to window cleaners. The dirt collects on the wiper blades when you drive in the rain, and even after you have cleaned the windshield the blades will streak it. Sprinkle a little nonabrasive cleanser on a wet sponge and wash the windshield and the wiper blades. Nine times out of ten, the streaking problem will be solved.

WAXING

The variety of car waxes on the market and the maker's claims for their performance is enough to send the average car owner into a frenzy of indecision (Fig. 3-2). Most, if not all of them, are quite good, and you will probably decide which one is best for you from your own experience. An old rule of thumb stated that the harder wax was to work with, the better it protected. It appears as though technology has changed all that. Most modern waxes are easy to work with and provide excellent protection. Regard claims for miracle cleaner waxes that last for nearly ever with a little intelligent skepticism. Ask someone who has used the product before you invest in it.

Fig. 3-2. A variety of cleaning and waxing products.

Always wax your car in the shade regardless of what the maker might have to say about waxing in the sun. Make sure the car is clean and free of dust. Waxing a dusty car will only succeed in scratching the paint. Otherwise, follow the instructions on the can. Badly faded paint can be restored with cleaner wax or a fine grit rubbing compound. You can use cleaner wax on lacquer or enamel. Before you use a rubbing compound on your car, find out whether it is painted with lacquer or enamel. Enamel rubbing compound is finer, less abrasive than the lacquer compound. You can use enamel compound on lacquer, but you shouldn't use lacquer compound on enamel.

INTERIOR CARE

A clean, well maintained interior adds value to your car and makes driving it more pleasant. There's nothing warmer, more comfortable, or more luxurious than velour seats, but they are difficult to keep looking their best. If you cover them with plastic, you defeat all reason for having velour. The best way to clean a velour seat is to keep it from getting dirty in the first place. You can clean lightly soiled velour with any good household upholstery cleaner or with a cleaner made especially for velour. Severe soiling or stubborn stains should be left to a professional upholstery cleaning company.

Leather upholstery has practically disappeared from American cars, and more's the pity. It is elegant, comfortable, and extremely durable. It has, however, become prohibitively expensive. Cowhide is the most common, and you will find it in a variety of grades. Clean your leather upholstery with a good quality saddle soap according to the instructions on the can.

Vinyl under the trade name Naugahyde became popular with the custom car builders in the fifties. The best quality vinyl looks and feels like leather, but it is tougher and easier to care for. Generally, you can clean your vinyl seats with ordinary household soaps or detergents. Very harsh cleaners will harm vinyl, but otherwise almost anything will do. Special vinyl cleaners help preserve the natural shine, and there are a variety of treatments available to restore the luster to worn vinyl. Torn seams and cuts in the material are about the only real problems with vinyl.

You should care for the carpeting in your car in the same way you care for the carpeting in your living room. It's probably made from the same material. Vacuum your car carpets about as often as you vacuum household carpets. Use a high performance industrial vacuum cleaner or one of the ones that you find outside coin operated car washes. The small pebbles and heavy grit in the carpet will damage household vacuum cleaners.

Shampoo the carpet at least once a year with any good household carpet cleaner. If you put floor mats down to protect the carpet, make sure that you don't allow moisture to collect under them. Mildew will grow and eventually rot the carpet fibers.

DEGREASING THE ENGINE COMPARTMENT

A clean engine compartment lends a certain amount of credibility to your attitude about car care. You'll see it reflected in the eyes of the dealer's appraiser at trade-in time. A clean engine compartment shows that you really care about your car. If you begin an annual engine cleaning program early in the car's life, you will find that the job is quick and easy.

First remove the air cleaner as shown in Fig. 3-3. Unscrew the wingnut, remove the top, disconnect the hoses, and lift the as-

Fig. 3-3. Remove the air cleaner.

sembly from the carburetor. Cover the carburetor with a heavy plastic food storage bag and secure it with a rubber band. Disconnect the high tension leads from the spark plugs and label them accordingly. See Fig. 3-4. Counting from the front nearest the radiator to the back, in-line engine cylinders are arranged 1 through 4 or 6. Counting from the front, cylinders numbered 1 through 3 or 4 are on the right bank as seen from the driver's seat of Ford V6 and V8 engines. Four through 6 or 5 through

Fig. 3-4. Label the disconnected spark plug wires.

8 are on the left. The odd numbered cylinders 1, 3, 5, 7 are on the left bank as seen from the driver's seat of most General Motors and Chrysler V8 engines. Two, 4, 6, and 8 are on the right, and the lowest number is always up front nearest the radiator. Some General Motors cars are the reverse, with the odd number cylinders on the right bank.

Trace each spark plug wire back to the distributor and label the socket with the corresponding number as shown in Fig. 3-5. Remove the coil lead from the center of the distributor cap and cover the distributor with a plastic bag secured with a rubber band.

Spray a warm engine with an engine degreaser, and pay special attention to areas where dirt and oil have built up into a thick sludge. Let the degreaser sit for 15 to 20 minutes, then rinse the engine with cold water under high pressure. Degreaser works best on a warm engine, but you should never use it on a hot engine. Let the engine dry for 15 minutes or so, dry the spark plugs with a clean absorbent cloth, reconnect the plug and coil wires and replace the air cleaner. Start the engine and check to see that everything is working correctly.

Engine degreaser will kill grass and soften asphalt driveways. If you degrease your engine while the car is parked on the lawn, expect a large brown area where the grass used to be. If you

Fig. 3-5. Label the distributor sockets.

do it in the driveway, rinse the driveway down thoroughly after you have finished rinsing the engine.

RUST PROOFING

If you live in an area of the country where ice and snow covered roads are treated with salt, you might want to consider one of the rust proofing treatments for your car. Rust inhibiting coatings sold under trade names such as Ziebart, Dura-Coat, Tuff-Kote, and Rusty Jones are sprayed into virtually every nook and cranny including the insides of doors and body panels. For the most part, all of them work very well, and they are certainly better than conventional undercoating.

Before you decide which one of the treatments to buy for your car, examine the manufacturer's claims, guarantees, and talk with people who have used the product for at least the life of the maker's guarantee. These treatments are expensive, and if you plan to keep your car for a long time, it pays to choose carefully.

CHAPTER 4

Tires and Wheel Bearings

Tires and wheel bearings generate quite a lot of your car's rolling friction. In light of the ever increasing gasoline prices and the ever decreasing supply, it makes sense for you to pay close attention to the condition of these components. Their condition affects the car's safety as well. Badly worn tires puncture more easily than ones with sufficient tread depth, and they offer little traction on wet roads. Dry wheel bearings might seize on the spindle, snap it off, and send the wheel scurrying off down the road independent of the car.

TIRES

Think of your tires as four separate contact patches roughly 64 square inches each. (Some are larger, some are smaller). Those four patches of rubber are really all that hold your car to the road. They provide the traction needed for acceleration, braking, cornering, and straight line directional stability.

Under the ideal conditions of smooth dry pavement, a straight stretch of road, and moderate speed, just about any tire that fits on the rim will suffice. When you add bumps, holes, lateral and longitudinal ridges and grooves, rain, a variety of pavement surfaces, corners, braking, acceleration, and high speeds, you begin to realize just how important these four contact patches are. As far as I can determine, there is no justification for taking the quality and condition of tires any way but seriously.

Years ago, choosing tires for your car was a simple process. You had to consider the size, white or black wall, conventional or mud and snow, and the price. Technology has changed all that. Balanced against how much you can afford to spend for a set of tires, you now have the opportunity to consider bias-ply, bias-belted, radial-ply, load range, tread design, tread compound, profile ratio, white stripe, black wall, raised white lettering, speed rating, guaranteed mileage, and the manufacturer's warranty against defects in workmanship and materials, and his warranty against road hazards. The list of alternatives is staggering.

Bias-Ply Tires

Bias-ply tires have been with us for a long time, and until fairly recently, they have been the most popular. Bias-ply describes the construction of the tire's carcass. Layers of reinforcing cords running from bead to bead cross one another usually at a 35 degree angle from the center line of the tire (Fig. 4-1). Bias-ply tires are strong and flexible, while they provide a soft quiet ride. Their biggest advantage, however, is also their greatest weakness.

Bias Ply Tire	Belted-Bias	Radial

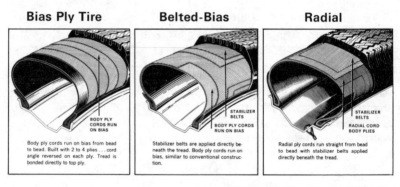

Body ply cords run on bias from bead to bead. Built with 2 to 4 plies . . . cord angle reversed on each ply. Tread is bonded directly to top ply.

Stabilizer belts are applied directly beneath the tread. Body ply cords run on bias, similar to conventional construction.

Radial ply cords run straight from bead to bead with stabilizer belts applied directly beneath the tread.

Courtesy Firestone Tire and Rubber Co.
Fig. 4-1. What's inside a tire.

The flexibility built into the bias-ply passenger car tire that gives you the quiet comfortable ride also allows the tread to distort during braking, acceleration, and cornering. Even in a straight line, the tread squirms and pinches together. This squirming hastens wear and reduces traction. Tire makers can eliminate most of the squirm by changing the cord angle and by using stiffer cords. That's the way racing tires are built, but the increased ride harshness would be unacceptable to a majority of drivers.

Because of the overall flexibility, bias-ply tires react strongly to longitudinal ridges, grooves, trolley car tracks, and low road shoulders. Place a pair of wheels on trolley car tracks imbedded into the pavement, and you can feel the car dart one way then the other as the tire's tread and carcass react to the irregularity. If you place one or two wheels off the pavement onto a low shoulder and try to steer back onto the road without slowing to a crawl, the tire's reaction can be violent enough to wrest control from your hands. Tread distortion during braking, acceleration, and cornering reduces traction on both wet and dry pavement. Bias-ply tires don't wear all that well and these days rank as merely adequate tires. A cynic might call them rim protectors.

Bias-Belted Tires

Bias-belted tires are simply bias-ply tires with a reinforcing belt placed around the circumference of the tire between the tread and the carcass. See Fig. 4-1. Cord angle and general construction are the same as the bias-ply tire, and the belted tire shares the same ride characteristics with perhaps a slight increase in harshness over small road surface irregularities. The reinforcing belt prevents the tread from distorting during braking, acceleration, and cornering and generally provides the tire with excellent traction. The belt also decreases rolling friction, reduces squirm, and increases the tire's tread life. Bias-belted tires react to longitudinal ridges in much the same way as ordinary bias-ply tires do. These tires are normally priced between bias-ply and radial-ply, and rank a cut above the bias-ply tire.

Radial-Ply Tires

Radial-ply tires have been used in Europe since shortly after World War II and have been popular there since the fifties. Anyone who has been interested in European cars, especially the high performance sports cars, knows and appreciates the radial tire's advantages over bias or bias-belted tires. Only during the seventies, however, have the majority of American drivers learned to understand and respect the performance benefits of radial tires. Radials are now standard equipment on many domestic cars.

The cords of the radial tire's carcass run across the tire and join the bead at right angles. One or more steel or fabric belts placed around the tire's circumference between the tread and carcass reinforce the tread. See Fig. 4-1. The design combines an extremely stiff tread with soft flexible side walls. Under the most severe cornering, braking, and acceleration loads, the tread remains essentially undistorted and keeps all or most of its contact patch firmly planted on the road surface. The tread does not pinch together and close off the rain sipping grooves cut into it, and the tire returns better wet road traction as a result. The rigid tread surface accounts for the low rolling friction, excellent steering response, and excellent traction normally associated with radial tires. The soft side walls flex to absorb large road shocks.

Because the tread is virtually distortion free, it will last up to twice as long as that of a bias-ply tire. Many radial tire makers guarantee their tires for forty thousand miles of wear under normal driving conditions. Radial tires cost more than the other types discussed, and sometimes nearly twice as much as an average quality bias-ply tire. But the increase in tread wear, the fuel economy advantage of lower rolling resistance, and the tire's superior handling traits more than make up for the higher purchase price.

In the past, radial tires have been noisy, and certain high performance radials still tend to hum or whine at highway speeds. Many of them, especially the European steel belted tires, ride harshly over small and relatively sharp road irregularities such as expansion strips in concrete highways. That harshness has been tuned out of most American built radials and many of the European textile belted tires. Usually, the textile belted tires ride better than the steel belted tires, but the steel belts offer better puncture protection. Most radial tires ignore longitudinal road irregularities such as trolley tracks, and you can put a wheel off onto the shoulder and steer the car back onto the pavement with virtually no protest or loss of control.

Because radial tires provide quicker steering response than bias or bias-belted tires, you should install them in complete sets. If you can't afford a complete set, buy at least two radials and put them on the rear wheels.

Tire Sizing and Rating

Unless you have followed the trends, tire sizing and rating can be confusing. Years ago, American tires stated size this way, 7.75x14. The tire in question was 7.75 inches wide and fitted a 14 wheel. In the late sixties, things changed. Low profile tires similar in appearance to racing tires became the rage, and a new twist was added to the sizing.

These bias-belted, low profile tires were labeled F70x14. "F" indicates the width (7.75), 70 indicates that the height of the tire from rim bead to tread is 70% of the tire's width (previously all tires had a height that was 83% of the width), and 14 indicates the diameter at the rim bead. Tires are now available in 78, 70, 60, and 50 series profile ratios and a variety of widths from A to N. Choose tire widths wisely. Be sure that they aren't too wide for the wheels, or if you buy wider wheel and tire combinations that they aren't too wide to clear the inner and outer fenders at full steering lock and full suspension compression. When you change the profile ratio and/or tire width, you also alter the car's handling characteristics, and it is a good idea to buy the tires in complete sets.

European radials have always carried metric sizing such as 155Rx15. The first three digits indicate the width in millimeters,

"R" means radial, and 15 indicates the diameter in inches. Along with the width in millimeters, you might find the letters SR, HR, or VR. For example, a 185HR14 tire is 185 millimeters wide, has an H speed rating, is a radial, and is 14 inches in diameter.

Speed ratings are determined by tests where the tire is run at its maximum designed speed under full load for 24 hours. "S" tires are capable of sustained speeds up to 113 mph, "H" tires to 135 mph, and "V" tires up to 165 mph.

Recently, European tire makers have begun including the profile ratios in their tire sizing, such as 225/60VR15, and the American manufacturers have begun using metric sizing, such as P205/70R14. The letter P in the P-series American metric radials indicates passenger car tire; 205 is the width in millimeters; 70 is the profile ratio; R indicates radial; and 14 is the diameter in inches.

Molded into the side wall of all Department of Transportation approved passenger car tires you will find the maker's maximum load and pressure recommendations. For example, 1050 lbs. at 36 psi means that each tire is capable of supporting 1050 lbs. at an inflation pressure of 36 pounds per square inch at a certain maximum speed for an indefinite period of time.

The strength of the tire is determined in large part by the number of cord plys or layers used to construct the carcass. Some time ago, tires had 4, 6, or 8 plys, and each was able to carry a certain load. The more plys, the heavier the load carrying capacity. Improvements in tire cord technology have allowed manufacturers to reduce the number of carcass plys while maintaining the strength. For example, a tire with 2 cord plys is as strong as a tire that once needed 4 plys. A 2 ply tire can have a 4 ply rating, and the maker states this as load range B. Load range C indicates 6 ply rating, load range D indicates 8 ply rating.

Inflation Pressure

Printed on a decal affixed to the driver's door post or to the inside of the glove compartment door, you will find the manufacturer's recommendations for tire inflation pressure relative to loads carried and speeds driven. The figures are suggestions for the original equipment tires, and they are based upon data gathered during tests. The figures reflect compromises in ride, handling, and fuel economy, and they allow a margin of safety. You cannot go wrong if you follow these suggestions. Always check inflation pressure when the tire is cold, that is, before you have driven on it. Even a short drive will heat the tire up enough to give you an optimistic reading.

If your car has full coverage wheel discs, it will have an air valve extension that allows you to inflate, deflate, or check the pressure without removing a valve stem cap. Simply place the pressure gauge squarely on the stem and press firmly. You'll hear a short fffffftt which means that the pressure gauge has engaged the air valve. If air continues to leak around the gauge, it means that you haven't sufficiently seated the gauge. See Fig. 4-2.

Fig. 4-2. Checking tire pressure.

Why worry about tire pressures? Well, for one thing, under-inflated tires are dangerous. Rolling resistance increases as the inflation pressure decreases. A soft tire runs hotter as a result of the increased friction, and if you allow it to do so for a long stretch at highway speeds, the tread will begin to disintegrate. This is especially true if the car is heavily loaded or is towing a trailer with a heavy tongue load.

Underinflated tires transform a normally precise handling car into one that feels disconnected from the road surface and from the car's controls. Emergency maneuvers such as a sudden lane change to avoid a skidding car will take longer, and your control over the car will be hazardously poor.

A severely underinflated tire is dished in the center of the tread, and as a result, the outside edges of the tread will wear faster than the center. See Fig. 4-3. The increased rolling re-

Fig. 4-3. Underinflated tire.

Courtesy Firestone Tire and Rubber Co.

Fig. 4-4. Overinflated tire.

Courtesy Firestone Tire and Rubber Co.

sistance of an underinflated tire requires more power from the engine to drive the car at a given speed. Fuel economy suffers. An underinflated tire isn't able to absorb shock as well as one that is correctly inflated. Sharp edged pot holes will compress the tire into the rim, dent it, and damage the tire's carcass.

Overinflated tires, on the other hand, present fewer dangers than underinflated ones, and they tend to wear out faster in the tread center than at the edges. See Fig. 4-4. A car with modestly overinflated tires will steer more accurately and corner more assuredly, but the ride quality suffers. It is wise never to exceed the tire maker's suggested maximum inflation pressure printed on the side wall of the tire. Both overinflated and underinflated tires give up some of their contact patch area, and in both cases the tires will provide less traction. Radial tires are safer at under- and overinflation than are bias and bias-belted tires.

How will you know when a tire is going flat or is about to blow out while you are driving? If one of the front tires is losing air while you are driving, the car will pull to the side that is going flat. The pulling will be especially strong during braking. Unless you hit something that blows the tire out suddenly, you can usually feel a high frequency vibration in the steering wheel and hear a distinct humming before a front tire blows out. There is, however, no way to determine just how long after the feedback begins that the tire will blow.

A rear tire that's going flat will cause the car to squirm or wander from side to side as you drive it in a straight line. If a left rear tire is going flat and you are driving a left hand corner, the rear of the car will try to swing around, and the front of the car will veer toward the inside of the corner. A rear tire that's close to a blow out will hum, but you won't be able to hear it as easily as you did the front tire. You will feel no vibration in the steering wheel. Rear tire blow outs are more dangerous than front tire blow outs because the car tends to spin, tail out toward the side of the damaged tire. Although it's hard, you can still steer a car when one of its front tires blows out. Never brake hard after one of your tires has blown. Let the car coast to a stop.

When should you replace your tires with new ones? When the tread depth is only 1/16 of an inch, or when the tire is unevenly worn as a result of over- or underinflation, maladjusted wheel alignment, or poorly balanced tires.

WHEEL IMBALANCE

An unbalanced front wheel manifests itself in vibration through the steering wheel, and an unbalanced rear wheel transmits a low frequency vibration that you can feel through the seat. The condition is more annoying than dangerous, but if you don't have it corrected, the tires will become scalloped or cupped. See Fig. 4-5. Once the tire has reached this stage, it is suitable only for the trash. When you detect vibration through the steering wheel or the seat, have a competent tire shop, service station, or dealer check the wheels for balance. The cost is moderate, about seven dollars per wheel for high speed balancing, but the benefits are great. If wheel balancing doesn't stop the vibration, your car probably has a suspension problem.

WHEEL ALIGNMENT

Unless the error is gross and easily discernible just by looking at the angle of the wheel, or unless the car pulls to one side when you let go of the steering wheel, or unless the car weaves from

Fig. 4-5. Appearance of tire caused by suspension neglect.

Courtesy Firestone Tire and Rubber Co.

side to side as you try to drive in a straight line, alignment faults can't be detected without a professional checkup until it's too late to save the tires. That's where the error eventually shows up.

A narrow band of wear around the outside edge, roughly one third of the tread width, of one or both front tires indicates too much toe-in. Feathering over a large part of the remaining tread width usually accompanies the worn band. Feathering is a scuffing pattern where the tread bars wear on an angle toward the outside of the tire (Fig. 4-5). A similar band of wear and feathering sloping toward the inside of the tire indicates too much toe-out.

Toe-in means that the front wheels point in toward the center line of the car. It is as though the left front wheel were turning slightly right and the right front wheel were turning slightly left while the steering is centered and the car is being driven in a straight line. Toe-out is the opposite.

Camber is the angle of the wheel on a vertical plane from perpendicular to the road surface. Errors in camber, tilted too far in at the top (negative camber) or too far in at the bottom (positive camber) will wear a narrow band on the tread similar to the one caused by toe-in and -out. Usually, the condition takes longer to show up, and the worn band is not accompanied by feathering. Camber errors will change the handling characteristics of your car as well. You should have your car's front wheel alignment checked at least once a year.

Except for the 1963 through the current model Corvette, the 1979 Eldorado, Toronado, and Riviera, you should never have to think about rear wheel alignment. Rear drive American cars carry their differentials and axles in a rigid assembly that is secured to the chassis through a system of springs, shock absorbers, and locating links. The axle is positioned and mounted at the factory with the alignment set to specification. Unless something bends or breaks from abuse or an accident, the rear wheel alignment should never change. The new front-drive Citation, Phoenix, and Omega use a light tubular beam axle that is mounted to the chassis in a way that is similar to rear drive cars, and rear wheel alignment should never be a problem.

The four cars mentioned at the beginning of the prior paragraph, however, have independent rear suspensions. The Corvette's differential is bolted to the chassis, and it transmits power to the rear wheels through a pair of half axles. A universal joint at each end of the axles allows sufficient compression and rebound suspension travel. The Eldorado, Toronado, and Riviera are front drive cars, and their rear wheels are mounted to hubs that are attached to pivoting suspension control arms. Independent rear suspensions provide adjustments for toe-in, toe-out, and positive and negative camber. Tire wear patterns for misaligned rear wheels are similar to those associated with front wheels. You should have rear-wheel alignment checked at least once a year.

HOW TO CHANGE A WHEEL

Flat tires are a nuisance, and no matter how much you might wish otherwise, they almost always go flat when you are out on the road. Changing a flat along side the road can be frustrating and dangerous. Here are some rules by which you can abide and perhaps save yourself some grief.

1. Always carry a spare and check it frequently to see that it is properly inflated.
2. Carry flares or reflectors. Flares are best because they will warn oncoming traffic during the day as well.
3. Always carry a flashlight.
4. Always carry a jack and lug wrench and make sure they are in good condition.
5. Park your car as far off of the road as possible.
6. Avoid changing a wheel on soft and unstable surfaces.
7. Avoid changing a wheel on a steep incline.

Obviously, it's not always easy to find ideal surfaces for changing a wheel, and driving on a flat tire for any distance will ruin the tire. But if the alternative is a great risk to your safety, it seems to me that ruining the tire is better than ruining yourself.

Assuming that you have found a suitable spot for changing the wheel, first set up your flares or reflectors. Engage the handbrake and make sure that the transmission is in gear or "Park." Place blocks or wedges in front of and behind one wheel opposite the end of the car with the flat tire. Place the spare and your wheel changing tools on the ground near the corner of the car that has the flat tire. With the tapered end of your lug wrench or a screwdriver, pry the hubcap or wheel cover off (Fig. 4-6). Loosen the

Fig. 4-6. Removing the wheel cover.

lug nuts a couple of turns. If you cannot budge the nuts, position the lug wrench so that you can apply pressure with your foot as shown in Fig. 4-7. Make sure that the wrench fits squarely on the nut.

Set up your jack according to instructions in your owner's manual. Place it squarely on the ground and raise it until it just engages the car. If the car comes with a bumper jack, information in the owner's manual should tell you the best location along the bumper to place the jack. Usually opposite or near a bumper bracket is the best spot. When you are sure that everything is correctly placed, begin jacking up the car. See Fig. 4-8. As you raise the car, make sure that the jack remains securely positioned. Raise the car high enough so that the fully inflated spare will clear the ground.

Turn the hubcap or wheel cover upside down, remove the lug nuts, and place them in the wheel cover. Remove the flat and

Fig. 4-7. Loosening a stubborn lug nut.

install the spare. Replace the lug nuts and tighten them finger tight. You will notice the tapered end of the lug nuts; make sure that these tapers are seated into the wheel (see Fig. 4-9) before you lower the car. With the lug wrench, tighten each nut a couple of turns, then lower the car and remove the jack.

After you have lowered the car and before you do anything else, tighten the lug nuts as tightly as you can. Replace the wheel

Fig. 4-8. Unit construction jacking point.

Fig. 4-9. Make sure that the lug nut tapers are seated
before lowering the car.

cover or hubcap. You may have to pound it on with the heel of
your hand. Make sure that it's securely seated, otherwise the first
bumps will send it flying. Check the spare's inflation pressure,
then return the tools and the flat to the trunk. Extinguish the
flares, and you're ready to drive away. Don't forget to get the flat
tire fixed.

ROTATING YOUR TIRES

According to tire manufacturers, rotating your car's tires every
6 to 8 thousand miles will increase tread life by about 20%. This
is especially true of heavy, front drive cars where the tires have to
support 60% of the car's total weight, suffer most of the braking
load, and deal with steering and acceleration loads. Cornering
loads imposed upon the front tires by the front weight bias of
nearly every American car tend to wear them out along the outside third of the tread faster than over the remaining portion.

You should rotate your bias-ply tires according to the diagrams
in Fig. 4-10A. If you have a space saver spare or simply do not
want to include the spare in the rotation, follow the 4 wheel
plan. If your car is equipped with radial-ply tires, follow the 4
or 5 wheel radial tire diagram.

In order to rotate your tires, you will need a hydraulic floor
jack, four jack stands, and a lug wrench. Place a block in front
of and behind one of the front wheels, then position the floor
jack under the car's differential, as shown in Fig. 4-11. Raise the
car high enough so that the jack stands can be placed under the
rear axle, adjusted to a height that will allow the tires to clear

the floor by at least a couple of inches. Lower the car onto the stands. See Fig. 4-12.

When you want to raise the front of the car, place the floor jack at the center line of the car with the jack pad contacting the suspension cross member as shown in Fig. 4-13. Before you

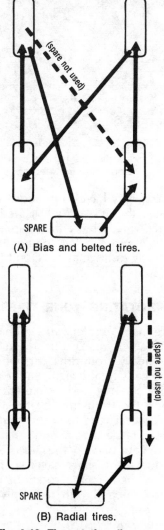

(A) Bias and belted tires.

(B) Radial tires.

Fig. 4-10. Tire rotation diagram.

begin jacking the car, make sure that the pad is not touching the engine oil sump. As you raise the car, the front wheels will drop until they reach the end of the suspension travel. Place your

Fig. 4-11. Place the jack pad under the differential housing.

Fig. 4-12. Place the jack stands under the axle.

stands under the chassis as shown in Fig. 4-14. After you have placed a pair of jack stands under both ends of the car, rock the car from side to side to make sure that it is secure on the stands. Rotate your tires according to the wheel changing instructions as shown in Fig. 4-10. Check the inflation pressures and adjust as necessary.

Fig. 4-13. Place jack pad on the front suspension cross member.

Fig. 4-14. Place jack stands under chassis near front of car.

WHEEL BEARING MAINTENANCE

Old timers and young men who have learned their craft from these men recommend that you or they repack your car's front wheel bearings every 10 thousand miles. These days, auto makers have extended that service to every 30 thousand miles. Perhaps you should strike a compromise at 15 thousand. Whatever you decide, wheel bearings do need periodic maintenance and adjustment if for no other reason than to cut rolling friction and improve fuel economy.

Front Wheels, Drum Braked Cars

Tools that you will need for repacking the wheel bearings include floor jack, two jack stands, lug wrench, large channel lock pliers, diagonal cutters, hammer, torque wrench and socket, and an 8-inch length of ½-inch hardwood dowel.

Jack up the car as has been described in the tire rotating section and be sure to block both rear wheels. Position the jack stands and lower the car onto them. Remove the hubcaps and both front wheels. Tap the spindle nut cover lightly all around with your hammer, then remove it with your channel lock pliers,

Fig. 4-15. Remove the spindle nut cover.

as shown in Fig. 4-15. Grip the head of the cotter pin with your diagonal cutters as shown in Fig. 4-16 and pull it out. Loosen the spindle nut with your channel lock pliers by turning it counter-clockwise, then remove it. Remove the outside bearing as shown in Fig. 4-17 and set it aside. Work the drum to and fro as shown in Fig. 4-18 until it is loose enough to pull off.

In the inside center of the drum assembly where it fits over the spindle, you will see a large grease seal. It seals grease in and dirt out, and you cannot remove the inner wheel bearing until you remove the seal. Place the drum, lug side up, on a bench. Insert the dowel into the drum assembly, as shown in Fig. 4-19. Position it on the outer ring of the bearing and tap the dowel rod with the hammer to remove the bearing and seal.

Fig. 4-16. Remove the cotter pin.

Fig. 4-17. Remove the outside wheel bearing.

Wash all surfaces and the bearings with a stiff brush and kerosene until all of the old grease has been removed. Shake the excess kerosene out of the bearings and set them aside to dry. Wipe all surfaces dry with a lint-free cloth.

Fig. 4-18. Jiggle the drum in and out and work it over the brake shoes.

Fig. 4-19. Use dowel rod to
remove inner bearing.

Fig. 4-20. Spread a finger full of grease on inside of spindle housing.

Use only high quality wheel bearing grease for repacking these bearings. NOTHING ELSE WILL DO! Spread a liberal amount of grease onto the inside surface of the spindle housing as shown in Fig. 4-20. Scoop up some grease with the first three fingers of your hand and press it or work it into the bearings, as shown in Fig. 4-21. Work it in until it oozes out the other side. Keep packing until you are sure the bearing will accept no more grease. Set the bearing in place and install a new seal.

Place the drum assembly open end up on a bench. Make sure that the seal seating area is clean, then set the seal in place. Make

Fig. 4-21. Work the grease into the bearing.

Fig. 4-22. Begin pressing in the new seal with your fingers.

sure that it sits squarely, then press it in all around the circumference with your fingers as shown in Fig. 4-22. With your hammer, gently tap one side then the next again and again until the seal's outer surface is flush with the metal housing. Pack the outer bearing and set it in place. You are ready to reassemble.

Clean the inside of the drum carefully with a brake cleaner. Avoid inhaling any brake shoe dust. It contains dangerous amounts of asbestos which is a proven carcinogen. Spray the brake cleaner inside the drum and wipe it dry with a cloth. Wipe the spindle clean, spread a coating of bearing grease over it, and replace the drum. You will probably have to wriggle the drum to and fro in order to work it over the brake shoes. Make sure the drum is fully seated, then replace the spindle nut. Tighten the spindle nut according to instructions in Wheel Bearing Adjustment Procedures at the end of this chapter. Install a new cotter pin and bend one end of it over the end of the spindle.

Wheel Bearings, Disc Brake Cars

Most of the procedure is the same as that used on drum brake cars except that in order to remove the brake disc assembly, you have to remove the brake caliper. The caliper and its anchor plate are attached to a backing plate behind the disc. Turn the steering wheel so that the caliper faces out. See Fig. 4-23 for caliper mounting bolt location.

Remove the bolts. They will probably be rusty and will need a thorough soaking with a penetrating oil. Give the penetrating

Fig. 4-23. Remove the caliper by removing the mounting bolts.

oil about ten minutes to work, then use your breaker bar and socket to get the bolts loosened. Finish removing them with your ratchet and socket.

After you have removed the bolts, lift the caliper clear of the disc. Insert a piece of wood or rigid cardboard that is at least as thick as the brake disc between the brake pads. If you don't do this, normal hydraulic system pressure will slowly but surely bring the pads together. When that happens, you have to remove

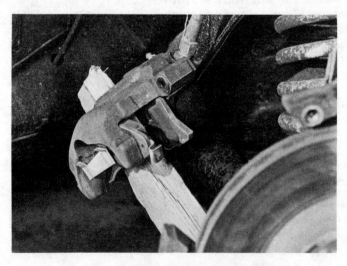

Fig. 4-24. Hang the caliper out of your way.

most of the brake fluid from the reservoir before you can safely pry the pads apart. In many cases, this procedure allows air to enter the system, and you will have to bleed it after you have finished the job. Bleeding the hydraulic system is best left to a professional mechanic.

Fashion a hook at both ends of a straight length of coat hanger and hang the caliper from a suspension part, as shown in Fig. 4-24. Following the instructions from the drum brake section, repack your wheel bearings.

Wheel Bearing Adjustment Procedures

1. *American Motors*—Tighten the spindle nut to 20-25 foot-pounds while rotating the wheel. Loosen the nut ⅓ of a turn then retighten it to 12 inch-pounds for models through 1973, and 6 inch-pounds for 1974 and later. Twelve inch-pounds is approximately finger tight. If you don't have an inch-pound torque wrench, finger tight will suffice.

2. *Chrysler Corporation*—All models through 1972. Before installing the adjusting nut lock, rotate the wheel and tighten the adjuster nut to 90 inch-pounds. Place the lock over the nut and make sure that one pair of slots lines up with the cotter pin hole. Back the assembly off one slot, and install a new cotter pin. Clean the grease cap and spread a thin coat of bearing grease on the inside. Replace the cap.

1973 and later models. Remove the nut lock and loosen the adjusting nut. Rotate the wheel while you tighten the adjuster nut to 20-25 foot-pounds. Loosen the nut a half turn or so, then retighten finger tight or so that one of the slots lines up with the cotter pin hole. Install a new cotter pin.

On some Chrysler Corp. models, you will find a lock nut in place of the nut lock. When you install the lock nut, be sure that you don't snug it up to the adjuster nut and tighten the adjuster nut with the lock nut. Install it so that the cotter pin slots line up with the pin hole and the lock nut is in contact with the adjusting nut.

3. *Ford Motor Company*—All models 1972-1979. Loosen the adjusting nut three turns. If your Ford has disc brakes, rock the disc rotor to and fro to make sure that the brake pads clear the rotor. Tighten the adjusting nut to 17-25 foot-pounds. Loosen the nut ½ turn, then retighten to 10-15 inch-pounds (finger tight). Install the lock nut and a new cotter pin.

4. *General Motors Corp.*—Front wheel bearings all models from 1972-1979 except Cadillac and Seville, Eldorado, Oldsmobile, Cutlass, Omega, Starfire, and Toronado.

Tighten the spindle nut to 12 foot-pounds while rotating the wheel forward. Loosen the nut by ¼ to ½ turn, then retighten it finger tight. Loosen the nut until the nearest spindle hole lines up with the slots in the castle nut. Install new cotter pin.

Cadillac and Seville. Tighten the spindle nut to 15 foot-pounds while rotating the wheel forward. Loosen the nut until it is free, then retighten finger tight. If the castle nut slots don't line up with the spindle holes, loosen the nut until the nearest hole does.

Eldorado. Tighten the spindle nut to 15 foot-pounds while rotating the wheel forward. Loosen the nut about one flat or until it is just loose. Tighten finger tight and install a new cotter pin.

Oldsmobile, Cutlass, Omega, Starfire. Tighten the spindle nut to 30 foot-pounds while rotating the wheel forward. Loosen the nut by ½ turn, then snug it up finger tight. Install the cotter pin or retaining ring. If you cannot install the cotter pin, loosen the nut until the slot lines up with the serrations on the nut. Oldsmobile recommends that you do not back the nut off more than ¹⁄₂₄ of a turn. Toronado front wheel bearings do not require adjusting or lubrication. They have to be replaced as a unit when they wear out.

Toronado Rear Wheel Bearings. The real wheel bearings on the Toronado are virtually identical to the front wheel bearings on rear drive cars. Refer to front wheel bearing service discussed earlier in this chapter. After service adjust as follows. While rotating the wheel forward, tighten the spindle nut to 25-30 foot-pounds. Loosen the nut ½ turn, then finger-tighten it. If the castle nut slots don't line up with the pin hole, loosen the nut to the nearest slot.

Eldorado Rear Wheel Bearings. Service them as you would most front wheel bearings. Cadillac recommends repacking these bearings with a high melting point, grade 2 lithium grease. For 1972 models, spin the wheel as fast as you can while tightening the spindle nut to 15 foot-pounds. Loosen the nut until it is free, finger-tighten it, and insert the new cotter pin. If neither of the two pin holes in the spindle lines up with a castle nut slot, loosen the nut until the nearest one does. If your car is equipped with Track Master, insert the pin into the end of the sensor assembly with pliers and install the insulators on each end of the pin. Be sure the pin protrudes an equal amount from either end.

1973 and later model Eldorados. Spin the wheel as fast as you can while tightening the spindle nut to 25-30 foot-pounds. Loosen the nut ½ turn and tighten it to 24 inch-pounds. Install the new cotter pin.

CHAPTER 5

Brakes

Your car's brakes are its first line of defense, and you should never take the system for granted. The rate at which your brake shoes or disc pads wear depends upon how and where you drive. Experts consider 12 to 15 thousand miles a year in mixed traffic conditions as average use, and an annual brake inspection should prove adequate. If you drive twice that distance but mostly on interstate highways, an annual inspection will suffice. If you drive daily in heavy stop and go traffic, take occasional highway trips, but never exceed 12 thousand miles, one inspection a year will be enough. Double the heavy traffic mileage, and you should check lining wear twice a year. Drivers who wait until the last minute to brake for traffic lights or what-have-you should inspect the brakes on their cars more frequently than the mileage would indicate.

Periodic inspection and maintenance is always the best medicine. Conscientiously applied, such a program will prevent expensive repairs and practically eliminate the possibility of brake failure. Ignore the system and linings will wear out. The hydraulic system might develop leaks, and one day you will find yourself without brakes.

Brake maintenance and repair is messy, time consuming, and frequently difficult. Many of the procedures require special tools, and any brake work including inspection demands the utmost care. A mistake can endanger your life and the lives of those who share your car and the lives of drivers who share the road with you. In the interest of everyone's safety, we will confine our discussion to operating principles, inspection, and symptoms associated with deteriorating or failing brakes.

THE HYDRAULIC SYSTEM

Your car's hydraulic system contains a master cylinder, a vacuum operated power booster, a proportioning valve, a metering valve, wheel cylinders, and/or calipers. Not all cars will have all of these components. The entire system from master cylinder to wheel cylinders is filled with hydraulic fluid and sealed with O-rings, seals, and tapered fittings, and should be air-free.

When you step on the brake pedal, a plunger connected to the pedal arm acts on a piston in the master cylinder. The piston pushes fluid ahead of it and builds up pressure in the lines. The sudden increase in pressure forces a pair of brake shoe actuating pins outward against the brake shoes, as shown in Fig. 5-1. The pins push against the shoes and move them out into contact with the brake drum.

PROPORTIONING VALVE

Most cars equipped with disc brakes in front and drums in the rear, or disc brakes at both ends have a proportioning valve installed in the hydraulic line to the rear brakes. Front engined

Fig. 5-1. Wheel cylinder pins force the brake shoes into contact with the drum.

cars carry between 55 and 60 percent of their total weight over the front wheels. Under braking, more of the weight transfers to the front and unloads the rear wheels even more.

The proportioning valve is adjusted to compensate for the weight transfer, and it limits the amount of hydraulic pressure applied to the rear brakes. When it is working correctly, it prevents the rear wheels from locking before the front in an emergency stop. During normal stops, it allows both sets of brakes to work evenly relative to their loads. Ideally, the valve should be adjusted so that during an emergency stop, all four wheels lock at the same time. The valves are not field serviceable and have to be replaced when they malfunction.

METERING VALVE

Installed in the line to the front brakes of some cars is a metering valve that delays pressure to the front brakes on application. It reduces front brake pressure until pressure to the rear brakes builds up enough to overcome the return springs. The valve provides better balanced braking during mild stops, and it reduces front disc pad wear by preventing the discs from shouldering most of the braking load when operating line pressure is low.

A simple test will tell you that your metering valve is working correctly. Start the engine so that the power brake booster will work. Now gently apply the brakes. After about one inch of travel, you should feel a slight change in the pedal effort . . . like a bump or hesitation. That change indicates that the valve is working. If you don't feel the bump, have a professional mechanic check it out for you.

DISC BRAKES

Caliper disc brakes have been with us for a long time. They appeared on the 24 Hours of LeMans winning D-Type Jaguars in the mid fifties, and a few years later, Jaguar introduced them on their production cars. During the early sixties, disc brakes began showing up on small inexpensive sports cars, and not long afterward, they became standard equipment on some of the more mundane economy cars. American auto makers offered disc brakes as optional equipment during the mid sixties, and in 1966, Chevrolet offered them as standard equipment on all four wheels of the Corvette.

Why disc brakes? Well, for racing cars, they offered a degree of fade resistance and dependability under stress that engineers only dreamed about before. The brakes are self adjusting, and mechanics could replace pads during endurance race pit stops much more quickly than they could replace brake shoes. The driver discovered that the amount of pressure applied to the brake pedal was more directly proportional to the amount of pressure applied to the brake's friction surface. He could more easily modulate his car's braking. Because the pads maintain an almost negligible contact with the disc, the friction surface stays clean and dry. As a result, braking in the rain is more even and predictable.

Although you will never demand as much af your car's brakes as a racing driver does, you can enjoy the design's advantages. Except for the quick and easy pad changes which are common on racing brakes but sadly absent from most ordinary passenger car disc brakes, the benefits are the same. Here's how the brake works. A disc or rotor as it is sometimes called rotates freely on a spindle. A caliper is attached to an anchor plate which is in turn bolted to the spindle assembly. Housed within the caliper and secured with clips of one sort or another are a pair of friction pads. See Fig. 5-2. When you step on the brake pedal, pressure

Fig. 5-2. Disc and caliper. The screwdriver indicates
the inside friction pad.

in the system acts on one or more pistons to force the pads out and into contact with the disc rotor. They pinch the rotor. When you release the pressure, the pads retreat. There are no return springs.

Some calipers are fixed and have movable pistons on both sides. Other calipers have a single moving piston and floating or sliding caliper bodies. The inside piston pushes against the rotor and pulls the caliper body and stationary pad toward the center of the car and into contact with the rotor.

DRUM BRAKES

Considered obsolete by many, drum brakes have been around almost since the beginning of automotive history, and they are still used on the rear wheels of most cars available in the U.S. They are less expensive to produce than disc brakes, and they have been refined to give one time braking efficiency almost equal to a disc brake system. In order for an all drum system to perform as effectively as an all disc or a disc/drum system during repeated and extremely hard use, the drums have to be made excessively large and from expensive lightweight metal that can dissipate heat faster than cast iron.

Without power assist, however, the drum brake as we know it today has one advantage over the disc brake . . . reduced pedal pressure. In the early 1920's, Bendix invented the duo-servo drum brake system. The bottom of the forward facing shoe and the bottom of the rearward facing shoe are connected by a spring and an adjusting screw. As you apply the brakes, the wheel cylinder pins force the shoes out into contact with the inside surface of the brake drum. See Fig. 5-1.

The top portion of both shoes nearest the wheel cylinder actuating pins contacts the rotating drum first. Friction tends to rotate the shoes forward along with the drum. When that happens, the front shoe acting through the adjusting screw forces the bottom of the rear shoe hard against the drum. An anchor pin at the top of the backing plate stops the rear shoe from rotating around with the drum and applies a counter pressure to the front shoe. Simply stated, the drum's rotation helps apply the brakes.

The servo action or self-energizing makes it more difficult for the driver to modulate the braking force at the brake without rapid pumping. Accurate modulation of power drum brake systems is almost impossible. The only real advantages that drum brakes offer are production cost and the ease with which engineers can provide for an effective parking/emergency brake. The latter consideration is why most cars still use drum brakes on the rear wheels. In order to provide an effective parking brake on rear wheel disc brakes, engineers have to add a small drum to the rotor assembly.

INSPECTION AND TROUBLESHOOTING

It is a good idea to check the hydraulic fluid level in the master cylinder about as often as you check the engine oil level, once every 1000 miles or so. Low fluid level on cars with drum brakes at all four wheels is the first indication of a leak in the system. Locate the master cylinder, remove the lid as shown in Fig. 5-3, and measure the level. The fluid should be just about even with the top of the reservoir or not more than ¼ inch below. Add the proper type of fluid as necessary.

Fig. 5-3. Removing the master cylinder cover.

As disc pads wear, the fluid level in the master cylinder will go down. The hydraulic fluid forces the pads out toward the rotor to compensate for wear. In other words, the brakes adjust themselves. This is a slow process, and the master cylinder shouldn't need topping up very often. If you have to add fluid every week or two, the system has developed a leak. Disc brakes require a special high temperature hydraulic fluid. You can use it in a drum brake system, but you cannot use fluid made for a drum system in a disc brake system. Consult your owner's manual or ask the parts counter person for the correct type of fluid.

HYDRAULIC SYSTEM LEAKS

Do not attempt to repair or replace any component in your car's hydraulic system. It is complicated, requires special tools, and a mistake could be fatal. You can, however, save the repair shop time and yourself money if you discover the source of the leak.

Usually, leaks develop at line joints, so begin at the beginning . . . the master cylinder fittings. Wherever oil seeps or leaks, you will find an accumulation of oily dust and dirt. If the leak is strong enough, the source will be washed clean by the flow. The source of a low pressure seep will remain dirty. If the area around the master cylinder fittings is dirty, look for clean spots that might indicate the source of a high pressure leak.

If you can't find any signs of a high pressure leak, degrease the master cylinder, wipe it dry, and drive the car for several miles in stop and go traffic. Examine the area around the fittings for fluid deposits that indicate seeping. In many cases, you can stop a seeping leak by tightening the fitting just a little, less than a quarter turn.

Cars equipped with disc brakes will have fittings at the metering or proportioning valves. Follow the hydraulic lines to these components (they are usually located under the car tucked away from harm behind frame rails or in driveshaft tunnels) and examine the fitting for leaks as described above.

Hydraulic fluid lines are usually made from aluminum tubing. At both ends of the car roughly 18 inches from where the lines enter the brake backing plates or disc calipers, you will find another joint and a length of braided flexible hose. The hose is there to follow the suspension movement. You may find leaks at either end of the flexible hose. See Fig. 5-4. Every now and again, the flexible hydraulic line will run afoul of a suspension part that chafes a hole through the hose wall. Examine the hoses carefully.

You might find fluid leaking from worn out seals in drum brake wheel cylinders. In order to inspect these, you have to remove the brake drum. Refer to Wheel Bearings in Chapter 4 for front drum removal details. Removing the rear drums is easy. Jack the car up and secure it with a pair of jack stands. See Rotating Tires for details. Remove the wheels. With a hammer, tap the drum solidly around the inner surface between the axle and the wheel studs as shown in Fig. 5-5. This should loosen the drum and allow you to wriggle it away from the linings. Examine the wheel cylinder for leaks. It should be dry. Excessive leaking will coat the drum and shoes with hydraulic fluid and make the brake useless.

Fig. 5-4. Leaks can develop at the joint between the metal and the flexible brake lines.

Disc brake calipers will develop leaks at the bleed fittings and at the line fittings. See Fig. 5-6. Leaks from either fitting will cover the caliper with hydraulic fluid. Eventually the fluid will find its way onto the disc and make the brake useless. Leaks can also develop inside the caliper's hydraulic piston. Broken or worn out seals will allow fluid to escape the caliper and flow onto the rotor and pads.

When you have found the leak or leaks, take your car to a professional mechanic for repairs.

POWER BRAKES

Vacuum boosted power brakes have been used on American cars for more than 20 years. At one time they were considered a luxury option, now it's hard to buy a car without them. The

Fig. 5-5. Tap the drum with a hammer to free it.

Fig. 5-6. Disc brakes can leak fluid at the bleed and line fittings.

hydraulic system used with power brakes works exactly the same way as does a manual or unassisted system. The vacuum booster merely helps the driver apply the brakes.

Here's how it works. A vacuum diaphragm and housing are located between the brake pedal arm and the master cylinder. A hose connects the housing to the engine's intake manifold, and it contains a check valve to prevent pressure in the manifold from entering the vacuum housing during periods of low manifold vacuum.

When you push the brake pedal down, you close off the vacuum source and allow atmospheric pressure to enter the housing on one side of the diaphragm. The increased pressure actually applies the brakes. When you release the brake pedal, vacuum is created on both sides of the diaphragm and springs return the diaphragm and master cylinder piston to the released position. If the vacuum system ever fails, the brake rod will butt against the master cylinder actuating rod and provide direct mechanical operation. The effort at the pedal will be substantially increased.

In order to easily check the operation of your booster, leave the engine off and pump the brake pedal several times or until it becomes firm. Keep a steady pressure on the brake pedal and start the engine. The pedal should depress slightly if the booster is working correctly. If it doesn't respond as described, consult a professional mechanic.

Another test. Open the hood of your car. Have another person start the engine, apply the brakes, and hold the pedal down. You should hear a fairly short duration hiss coming from the booster assembly (Fig. 5-7). If the hissing is steady and continues for some time, the booster unit is faulty and should be replaced.

Fig. 5-7. The power brake booster.

SYMPTOMS AND CAUSES—DRUM BRAKE SYSTEMS

1. Excessive pedal travel. May be caused by too much clearance between the brake shoes and the drum. Drum brakes on cars built since the mid sixties have a self-adjusting mechanism built into them. In order to adjust these brakes, reverse the car and apply the brakes. If the pedal travel doesn't decrease, repeat the procedure. If this procedure fails to decrease the pedal travel, the linings may be worn out.

   Remove the brake drums and inspect the linings (Fig. 5-8). Some linings are riveted to the metal backing, and if the lining is worn to within a half thousandth of an inch of any rivet, it should be replaced. Uneven wear indicates that the shoes haven't been centering themselves in the drum during braking or that the drum is out of round. In either case, consult a professional mechanic. Some brake shoes have the lining bonded to the metal backing. Replace these when the lining wears to within a half thousandth of the metal backing.

Fig. 5-8. Measuring brake lining thickness with an ordinary ruler.

A sticking self-adjusting mechanism will keep the brakes from adjusting. If the same symptom of too much pedal travel occurs first thing in the morning when you first apply the brakes and works normally the rest of the day, the residual pressure check valve in the master cylinder may not be holding sufficient line pressure.

2. Soft spongy feel at the brake pedal. When you push down on the brake pedal, it feels as though the pedal is pushing back. This symptom results from bent or distorted brake shoes, poorly centered shoes, or a drum that is too thin or cracked.

3. Brakes grab and create braking force out of proportion to the pedal pressure. This symptom may be caused by loose linings, incorrect linings, distorted shoes, poorly centered shoes, loose or distorted backing plate, and scored or out of round drums.

4. Car pulls or swerves to one side when you apply the brakes. That usually means that one brake is working more efficiently than the other or that one of them is grabbing. See Symptom 3. Additional causes include water on the linings, grease or brake fluid on the linings, or a sticking hydraulic wheel cylinder.

5. Vibration or pulsating from the brake pedal is caused by one or more drums out of round or a bent rear axle.

6. Scraping noise, squealing, and chatter may be caused by bent or damaged shoes, linings worn down to the metal backing, sand or other debris in the drums, cracked or grooved drums, broken shoe return springs, broken shoe hold-down pins or springs.
7. Brake pedal refuses to return to its normal position, travel becomes shorter and shorter. This is caused by weakened or broken return springs or a sticking wheel cylinder.
8. Brake drag on one or more brakes. On the rear, this may be caused by sticking parking brake cables or linkage. On all brakes, it can be caused by weakened or broken return springs, malfunctioning automatic adjusters, sticking wheel cylinders, and bent or distorted shoes.

SYMPTOMS AND CAUSES—DISC BRAKES

1. Fading brakes that require more and more pedal pressure to stop the car result from grease, oil, or hydraulic fluid on the disc and pads.
2. Brakes grab. Pads may be loose on their backing plates or the caliper might be loose on the anchor plate.
3. Pulling or swerving to one side during braking may be caused by loose pads, loose caliper, or a sticking caliper piston.
4. Vibrating or pulsating brake pedal is usually caused by a warped rotor.
5. Brake squeal can be caused by vibrating pads which in many cases is no cause for alarm. Scraping noise and chatter is probably caused by worn out pads where the metal backing plate is contacting the rotor.
6. Brake drag on one or more wheels is caused by a sticking caliper piston or swollen seal.

SYMPTOMS AND CAUSES
RELATED TO BOTH SYSTEMS

1. Excessive pedal travel. Caused by a leak in the system, boiling brake fluid (refer to fluid requirements mentioned earlier in the chapter), low fluid level, air in the system, weakened hoses that expand under pressure, improperly adjusted master cylinder or power boost push rod.
2. Spongy brakes can be caused by air in the system, weak and expanding hoses, boiling brake fluid.
3. Grabbing brakes may be the result of a corroded master cylinder bore, faulty power booster, or a binding linkage between the brake pedal and the master cylinder.

4. Pulling to one side can be caused by worn or damaged suspension parts as well as by problems in the brakes. See drum and disc symptoms for details.
5. Vibrating or pulsating brake pedal might be caused by loose or badly worn wheel bearings.
6. A brake pedal that won't return to the top of its stroke can be the result of swollen master cylinder caps or plugged master cylinder compensating ports.
7. All brakes drag. Master cylinder ports might be clogged, brake pedal linkage might be binding, or the rubber parts in the caliper or wheel cylinder may be swollen as a result of poor quality or contaminated brake fluid.
8. One dragging brake may result from loose or badly worn wheel bearings, or a pinched brake hose that permits **flow** under pressure but will not allow the fluid to return.

Remember . . . anytime you have reason to remove a brake drum, replace linings, or service the wheel bearings, it's a good idea to inspect and service, as necessary, any of the systems components. After you have had new pads or linings installed, avoid heavy braking for 1000 miles or so. You'll give the linings a chance to bed in and prevent glazing.

CHAPTER 6

Lighting, Fuses, and Windshield Wipers

The lighting systems in American cars are generally very dependable, but you are bound to experience burned out bulbs and blown fuses from time to time. One word of caution: if you discover a blown fuse, replace it; but if it blows again almost immediately, there is a short somewhere in the system. Your car's electrical system isn't all that complicated, and with help from a wiring diagram, you would probably be able to locate and repair the problem. The snag here is finding the wiring. A lot of the wiring is hidden behind panels, carpeting, and what-have-you. Let the experts in electrical systems deal with the wiring problems.

Replacing burned out bulbs, lenses, and blown fuses, however, is easy, and the job rarely takes more than a few minutes. The average American sedan or wagon has a large selection of lights. Some are there for safety, such as side marker, head, and taillights, and others such as dome, trunk, and engine compartment lights are there for your convenience. Instrument lighting is safety related, but that is an area that should be left to the electrical experts.

You should probably check your car's lighting system about once a month. Ask a friend, your husband, wife, son or daughter to turn on the lights, step on the brake pedal, activate the turn signals, etc. while you walk around the car to see that all of the lights are working. Drivers who live in states where the government requires one or two inspections a year might be tempted to leave the lighting alone until inspection time. Those people are fooling only themselves. Lights allow others to see you as much as they allow you to see.

REPLACING A BURNED OUT HEADLIGHT

Federally approved headlights for all cars sold in the United States are sealed beams. Lens, reflector, and filament are sealed into a single unit that must be replaced as such when the filament burns out. All cars have some sort of trim around the headlights that has to be removed before you reach the sealed beam retaining screws or springs. Look for any screws in the bezel that surrounds the headlights and remove them, as shown in Fig. 6-1. If your car has pop-up headlights or headlight covers, consult your owner's manual for information regarding how to keep them up or open when the lights are off.

The sealed beam is secured to its shell by a retaining ring. The retaining ring is held to the lamp shell by at least 3 screws or in some cases tabs and a spring. Remove only the screws holding the retaining ring as shown in Fig. 6-2. Do not disturb the head-

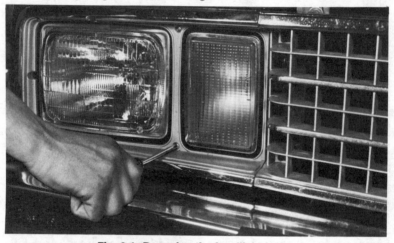

Fig. 6-1. Removing the headlight bezel.

Fig. 6-2. Sealed beam retaining ring secured with four screws.

light-adjusting screws. Remove the ring while you hold the sealed beam in place. In order to remove a retaining ring spring, grasp it with a pair of needle-nose pliers and pull it off the retaining hook.

Unplug the sealed beam from its socket, as shown in Fig. 6-3. Install a new sealed beam by reversing the disassembly order. Cars with two rectangular headlights require a number 2 sealed beam. Cars with four rectangular headlights require a number 2 sealed beam in the outboard sockets and a number 1 sealed beam in the inboard sockets. Before you replace the headlight trim, turn on the lights to make sure that the new beam is working.

Fig. 6-3. Unplug the sealed beam from its socket.

REPLACING BURNED OUT TAIL, STOP, TURN SIGNAL, AND BACK-UP LIGHT BULBS AND LENSES

Many modern cars house the tail, stop, turn signal, and back-up lights in a single large multisocket unit. In some cases, this large socket complex is covered by a single, multifaceted lens with its individual parts bonded together. Other light units may be covered by large multifaceted lenses with the individual parts held together by clips on the chrome divider strips. You might find retaining screws imbedded into the chrome perimeter trim, but in most cases, the entire light unit will be held in place from inside the trunk. Some auto makers provide access to the bulbs through holes in the body panel inside the trunk. See Fig. 6-4. Others require you to remove the entire light unit in order to reach the bulbs. See Fig. 6-5. Remove the rubber stud covers, remove the light unit retaining nuts, and remove the unit from the body to gain access to the taillight, turn signal, and back-up light bulbs.

Fig. 6-4. Remove taillight bulb from inside the trunk.

Most cars use a double-filament bulb for tail, stop, and turn signal lights. The smaller filament serves as the taillight, and the larger filament serves as the stop and turn signal light. Some other cars have totally separate turn signal lights usually covered by an amber lens, like many of the imported cars.

The double-filament bulbs have two pins spaced 180 degrees apart on the metal base. One pin is higher than the other, and these bulbs can be installed only one way. See Fig. 6-6. The pins have to match the grooves in the socket. In order to remove the bulb, push in and turn ¼ turn counterclockwise then pull it out of the socket. The pins are placed on the base, one higher than the other, to prevent anyone from reversing the filament connection at the base. Install the new bulb by reversing the removal procedure. Be sure to line up the correct pin with the correct

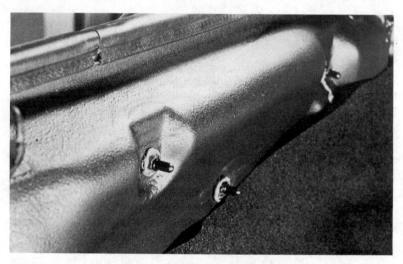

Fig. 6-5. Removing entire light unit.

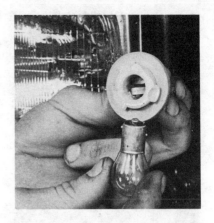

Fig. 6-6. Note the locating pins on the bulb case.

groove. Single-filament bulbs have the same two pins, but they are exactly opposite one another. They serve only to hold the bulb in the socket.

REPLACING A FRONT PARKING LIGHT BULB OR LENS

The parking lights on cars manufactured since 1968 stay on while the headlights are burning. The double filament bulbs are similar to the ones used for stop, tail, and turn signal lights. Generally, parking lights are separate from the headlight complex, and you may replace the bulb by removing the lens or removing the bulb and socket from behind the light. Examine the parking light for screws located at the lens perimeter. Removing these as shown in Fig. 6-7 will allow you to remove the lens and gain access to the bulb.

Fig. 6-7. Removing the parking-light lens.

REPLACING SIDE MARKER LIGHTS

You will find side marker lights alone on the fenders or as part of a wraparound parking light unit. You will be able to reach the bulb by removing the lens retaining screws and the lens, by pulling the bulb and socket out from inside the fender (see Fig. 6-8), or by removing the parking/side marker light assembly. Rear side marker lights may be part of a wraparound tail, stop, and turn signal assembly, and you will be able to reach the bulb from inside the trunk, as shown in Fig. 6-9.

Fig. 6-8. Front side marker light bulb socket. Twist socket ¼ turn counterclockwise and remove.

Fig. 6-9. Remove the rear side marker light from inside the trunk.

REPLACING LICENSE PLATE LIGHT BULBS AND LENSES

License plate lights are usually recessed into body panels or bumpers and located above, below, or at both sides of the plate. A chrome bezel and 2 screws may hold the lens in place or the lens may be screwed directly to the bumper or panel. Remove the screws, lift the bezel and lens away, and remove the bulb. See Fig. 6-10. Many of the small exterior lights use rubber gaskets around the lens to seal out water. When you are changing lenses or bulbs by removing the lens, be sure to replace the gasket and seat it carefully. Water in the bulb socket will corrode it and/or cause a short.

REPLACING DOME, TRUNK, AND ENGINE COMPARTMENT BULBS

Dome lights are covered by plastic lenses that either clip onto the light unit or are held in place by a couple of screws. See Fig. 6-11. Squeeze the snap-on lens together to free the tabs from

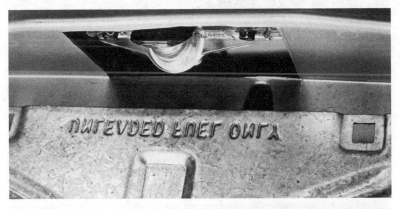

Fig. 6-10. Remove the license plate lens by removing the two ¼-inch hex head bolts.

Fig. 6-11. Remove dome light lens.

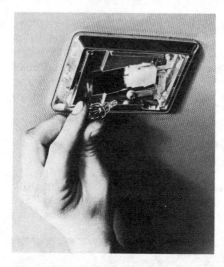

Fig. 6-12. This dome light bulb
looks like a flash bulb.

their slots and remove the lens. Some dome lights use bulbs that
look like large fuses or flash bulbs. See Fig. 6-12. Others use a
conventional push and turn bulb.

Trunk and engine compartment lights are not usually covered
by a lens. The bulbs will be either push and turn or fuse type.
See Fig. 6-13.

When you go to the auto parts store to purchase new bulbs,
always take the old one with you. It will save you and the counter
person time and ensure getting the correct bulb.

Fig. 6-13. Engine compartment light.

FUSES

The fuse panel on most American cars is located under the dash board on the driver's side. Sometimes it's near the center of the car and sometimes at the extreme left. Placement varies from model to model. A flashlight and a few minutes searching should produce your car's fuse panel. See Fig. 6-14. Automotive fuses protect your car's electrical system in the same way that household fuses or circuit breakers protect house wiring. If a malfunction overloads the circuit, the fuse blows and breaks the circuit before the wiring melts. Always use fuses of the correct amperage for the circuit and never substitute a length of wire for a fuse. Persistent fuse blowing indicates a problem in the system that needs the attention of a professional mechanic.

Fig. 6-14. Fuse panel located behind a decorative panel on the underside of the dash just to the left of the steering column.

Occasionally, a fuse will blow for no apparent reason; therefore, it's a good idea to carry a supply of assorted fuses in your glove compartment. Fuses are recessed into the panel, and it's almost impossible to remove them with just your fingers.

When a fuse blows, the components on that circuit will stop working. Locate the fuse panel. Usually the fuse sockets are labeled (see Fig. 6-14), and you should be able to locate the blown fuse by finding the one that corresponds to the circuit that has stopped working. The metal conductor in the fuse will be broken toward the center.

Before you attempt to replace the blown fuse, turn the ignition off. A good tool for removing fuses is a ¼-inch dowel sharpened at the end or a sharpened pencil. Reach into the panel at one end

Fig. 6-15. Removing a fuse with a pencil.

of the fuse and gently pry the fuse up and out, as shown in Fig. 6-15. Simply snap the new fuse into place.

TURN SIGNAL AND HAZARD WARNING FLASHERS

Turn signal and hazard warning flashers are small cylindrically shaped, solid-state devices that alternately break and complete the circuit and allow the lights to blink on and off. They are located under the dash or in the glove compartment. Some cars have them plugged into the fuse panel, others tape them to a section of the wiring harness, and on others you will find them secured to a panel by their own brackets.

Flashers are usually extremely dependable, but they can and do fail. Also, if you plan to tow a trailer, you might want to replace the flashers with heavy duty units that are designed to handle the extra load imposed on the flasher by the trailer lights. When a flasher fails, the hazard and turn signal lights will not work. One burned-out directional bulb will prevent that side from blinking.

Fig. 6-16. Locate the flasher unit.

The indicator light on the dash and the one good bulb will light, but will not blink.

Locate the malfunctioning flasher as shown in Fig. 6-16, remove the leads, and replace the flasher with a new one. When you buy a new one take the old one with you.

WINDSHIELD WIPERS AND WASHERS

Windshield wiper blades are squeegees that wipe water from the glass. The rubber is soft and pliable. It wears out, becomes

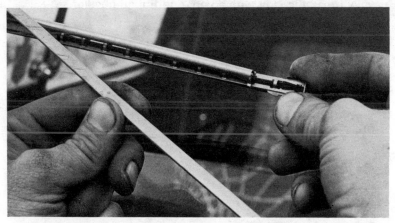

Fig. 6-17. Pinch the clip together and slide the blade from the holder.

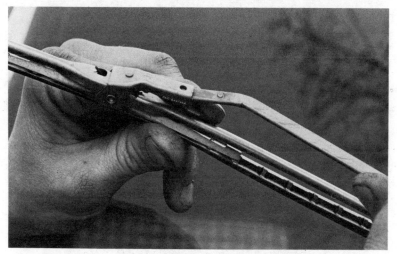

Fig. 6-18. To replace entire blade assembly, depress the tab (index finger) and release blade from wiper arm.

torn and frayed, and it becomes brittle from the effects of air pollution and salt and other road chemicals. Brittle or worn out blades streak the windshield and reduce visibility. See Figs. 6-17 and 18 for blade change details.

Dirty windshields are frustrating, and an empty washer reservoir even more so. Check the fluid reservoir anytime the hood is raised. Even if you live in year-around warmth, you should use some sort of washer detergent. It acts as a cleaner and an antifreeze. It is available premixed or as a concentrate. If the washer nozzle becomes clogged from car wax or other dirt, you can usually break the clog with a very fine-tipped needle.

CHAPTER 7

Battery, Belts, and Cooling Systems

Your car's lead-acid storage battery provides the amperage, up to more than 400 amps at 0 degrees F, that the starter motor needs to crank the engine. Because of the high amperage involved, corrosion, loose connections, and small electrical leaks from cracked insulation will make starting your car difficult. This is especially true when the temperature drops below freezing. The battery produces electricity from the chemical action between the sulfuric acid/water electrolyte and the lead compound plates. As the temperature drops, the chemical action slows down and weakens the battery.

When you turn the ignition key to "start," you complete a circuit from the battery through the switch, a relay and/or solenoid to the starter motor. The Bendix gear on the starter motor shaft engages the gear teeth on the engine's flywheel and cranks the engine at 180 to 250 revolutions per minute. Assuming that the car's secondary ignition system (coil, distributor, spark plug wires, spark plugs) and the fuel system are working correctly, the engine should start within several revolutions. Once the engine is running, alternating current, changed to direct current by the rectifier, from the belt driven alternator takes care of the car's electrical needs and maintains the battery's charge. A voltage regulator controls the amount of charge supplied to the battery.

The battery is the heart of the system, and it has to be kept in top condition at all times. The maintenance procedures are simple. Despite the fact that many drivers wait until the battery fails to start their cars before they consider its condition, a few simple tests that you can perform at home will allow you to monitor the battery's health and save you the grief of being stranded by battery failure.

A word of caution about battery maintenance. A by-product of the battery's chemical action is hydrogen gas. It is explosive. Keep all open flames away from the battery. Avoid making sparks when you are working on or near the battery. This is especially important when you are charging the battery because gasification increases.

The battery's sulfuric acid electrolyte is extremely corrosive. It will cause skin burns, eat holes in your clothing, and damage the car's painted surface. Protect yourself. Wear safety glasses when you add water to the cells or test them with a hydrometer. Protect the paint with a cloth or newspapers. If you splash any electrolyte on your skin, clothing, or the paint of the car, rinse immediately with cold clear water. If you splash the acid in your eyes, flush them immediately with cold water followed by a good eye wash followed by a visit to a doctor. The dirt, grease, and white scale found on the battery is contaminated with sulfuric acid. Wear gloves when you are handling the battery, and keep the battery dirt off your clothes and the car's paint.

Things that affect the health and life of the battery include a slipping alternator belt, faulty voltage regulator, faulty alternator, excessive cold, and most commonly, dirt, corrosion, and low electrolyte level.

Electrolyte is a mixture of water and sulfuric acid. The water in conventional batteries evaporates out of the solution and leaves a highly concentrated acid base that eats away at the cell material faster than a properly diluted solution. All that you need do to maintain the proper electrolyte level is top off each cell with distilled or deionized water. It's important to remember that ordinary tap water impurities will contaminate the electrolyte and reduce the battery's effective life span.

Remove the cell caps. They will either snap out or unscrew. Peer into each cell with a flashlight. The electrolyte should cover the top of the plates in each cell and be no higher than the split ring at the bottom of the filler neck. A good and safe way to add distilled water to the battery is with an ordinary kitchen basting syringe. Avoid overfilling. Wipe any spillage from the top of the battery and replace the caps. Check your battery's electrolyte level about once a month.

CLEANING THE BATTERY

The battery's acidic environment causes white scaly deposits to form and collect on both posts, but the condition is usually more severe on the positive post. See Fig. 7-1. If allowed to grow, the corrosion eventually works its way into the space between the

Fig. 7-1. Battery terminal corrosion.

battery post and the cable clamp where it acts as an electrical insulator. The deposits will also eat into the copper core of the cables, create excessive resistance, and eventually break the circuit.

Also, the dirt, grease, and scale that collect on the top of the battery case acts as a conductor and can cause an external short between the two posts. Begin by scraping the heavy deposits from the posts and clamps with a screwdriver or a small putty knife. Then mix your washing solution.

Add two tablespoons of baking soda to one quart of water and stir until all of the baking soda has dissolved. Dip a small brush such as a toothbrush into the solution and scrub the terminals. Do not allow any of the washing solution to enter the battery caps, because it will weaken the electrolyte. After the foaming has stopped, rinse the terminals with clear water.

Next, loosen the cable clamp pinch bolts with a wrench then remove each cable beginning with the negative (black) or ground cable. See Fig. 7-2. Removing the negative cable first will prevent sparking when you remove the positive cable. You won't always need to use a terminal clamp puller, but it is the safest and easiest way to remove the clamp from the post.

Now you are ready to remove the battery. The clamps that hold batteries into the box vary from model to model, but none are so complicated that you couldn't figure out the procedure after a little study. The battery clamp on some older cars may be so corroded as to render the thing useless for anything but the trash. Clean up the clamp well enough to remove it then replace it with a new one. The clamp and box are important. If the battery is

Fig. 7-2. Removing the negative cable with a terminal clamp puller.

allowed to move around in the box, the vibration and shock can break the plates or cause them to touch one another and destroy the battery.

Lift the battery out of the box. Automobile batteries are heavier than their size would indicate. Wear an old pair of work gloves to protect your hands from acid contaminated dirt, and be sure to lift the battery straight up and out. Tilting it too far will let acid spill out through the filler cap vents.

Place the battery on the garage floor near a drain or on the driveway. Wipe the cell caps clean with a cloth dampened in your washing solution then cover them with plastic wrap or aluminum foil. Scrub the entire battery with the washing solution and rinse with clear water. Set it aside to dry and go on to the battery box.

Scrape the heavy scale deposits off with a screwdriver or small putty knife. Scrub the box with your washing solution, rinse, and let dry. Remove peeling paint and heavy rust deposits with a stiff wire brush. Sand the entire box with a medium grit sandpaper, rinse the dust off with clear water, let it dry, and finish the job with a coat or two of rust inhibiting primer and top coat.

Before you return the battery to the newly refinished box, scour the posts and cable clamps with a terminal cleaning tool, as shown in Figs. 7-3 and 4. Insert the male end of the cleaner into the clamp and twist clockwise as you push it in and pull it out. Place the female end of the cleaner over the posts and twist clockwise while pushing it down. It's as though you were screwing the cleaner onto the post.

Fig. 7-3. Cleaning the battery post with the female end
of a terminal cleaning tool.

Inspect the clamps for cracks and examine the cables for broken core strands or cracked insulation. Place the battery into the box and secure it with the clamp. Place the positive cable clamp on the positive post and push it all the way down. You may have to tap it lightly a couple of times with a plastic mallet to seat the clamp. Tighten the clamp pinch bolt only tight enough to prevent the clamp from rotating on the post. If you snug it up too much, you might break the clamp. Install the negative cable in the same way.

Sometime during the life of your car you might have to replace a broken cable clamp or cut off the clamp and a badly corroded section of cable. New clamps are available from auto parts stores in kits such as the one shown in Fig. 7-5. If the cable is in good

Fig. 7-4. Cleaning the cable clamp
with the male end of the
terminal cleaning tool.

shape, cut the broken clamp off as close to the clamp as possible with your diagonal cutters. Strip a half inch or so of insulation from the cable as shown in Fig. 7-6 and bolt the new clamp to the bare cable.

Fig. 7-5. Typical battery cable clamp kit.

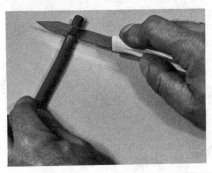

Fig. 7-6. Preparing a cable for a new clamp.

SPECIFIC GRAVITY TEST

Once or twice a year you should test the condition of the cells in the car battery with a hydrometer. Be sure to use a hydrometer that is made for testing only the specific gravity of batteries. Ideally, you should perform this test when the electrolyte is at 80° F. Measure the temperature by inserting an inexpensive Kodak photographic chemical thermometer into the cell. For every ten degrees above or below 80° F, add or subtract by a factor of 0.004. For example: if the electrolyte is 70° F and the battery is in excellent condition, the hydrometer should read 1.250 to 1.295 minus 0.004 or somewhere between 1.246 and 1.291.

A reading of 1.3 or higher at 80° F indicates that the specific gravity is too high. Adding a little distilled water should bring it down to normal. If the cell is already full, you can suck some of the electrolyte out with the hydrometer before you add the distilled water. A reading of 1.225 to 1.25 indicates fair condition, and any reading below 1.225 indicates that the cell is near death.

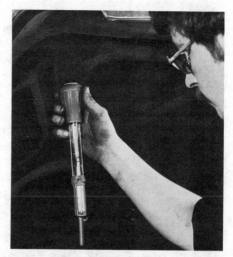

Fig. 7-7. Reading the battery hydrometer.

Remove the cell caps, and before you perform the test make sure that the electrolyte is at the correct level. Top up those cells that need it with distilled water then drive the car for about 15 minutes to ensure a thorough mix. Starting with the cell nearest the positive terminal, insert the hydrometer, squeeze the bulb slowly, then release it slowly. Lift the hydrometer from the cell (Fig. 7-8) and hold a cloth under it to absorb any acid drops. Hold the hydrometer as close to exactly vertical as you can and at eye level, then note the reading. Jot down each reading as you move along. A consistently fair to poor reading among all the cells may improve with a thorough charge. If one cell shows a reading of more than 0.025 lower than the others, that cell is dead or nearly so. You'll need a new battery. When you have finished the test, replace the cell caps and rinse the hydrometer with clear water.

If the specific gravity test indicates that your car battery needs charging, you can either take it to a service station or purchase a small charger and do it at home. Home use battery chargers are inexpensive, easy to use, and like adding water and cleaning the battery, they can help prolong the useful life of the battery.

First, clean the posts and cable clamps if they need it. Remove both cables, negative first, from the posts. Remove the cell caps. Because gasification increases during charging, always charge the battery in a well-ventilated area. Keep open flames and sparks away from the battery. Connect the negative charger clamp to the negative battery post. Connect the positive charger clamp to the positive battery post. Plug the charger in, set any dials according to the maker's instructions, and turn the charger on. The charge rate should not exceed 6 amperes. The battery will be fully charged when all the cells are gassing freely, and the specific gravity readings, at least three taken every hour, indicate no increase in specific gravity.

When you choose a new battery for your car, it is wise to pick one that is equal to or slightly more powerful than the one that came with your car. Skimping on power to save money is not always a good idea. Read the maker's warranty carefully, and shop around for the best combination of price, cranking power, and warranty. If you plan to keep your car for some time, you might want to consider one of the new sealed, maintenance-free batteries. The long life, excellent warranty, and dependability of these batteries more than compensate for the high price.

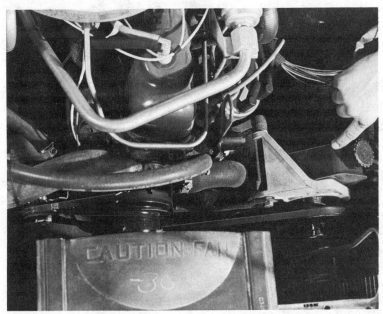

Fig. 7-8. Engine belts. Power steering indicated by finger.

BELTS

Some of your car's most important components such as the alternator, water pump, power-steering pump, and emissions-reducing air pump are driven by V belts from a pulley attached to the end of the crankshaft at the front of the engine. All American cars have at least one belt, and some have as many as three. See Fig. 7-8 for belt identification.

Usually, these belts are very durable, and with proper care, they should last for many thousands of miles. The belts are made from fiber-reinforced rubber, and they stretch very little. Adjustment, either too tight or too loose, oil, dirt, and age all work to shorten the belt's useful life. Adjusted too tight, the belt is subjected to a great deal of stretching force, an increase in friction, and heat, all of which combine to wear away the rubber and break the reinforcing cords.

Adjusted too loose, the belt slips and squeals under abrupt and hard acceleration, when starting a cold engine, or when the steering wheel is turned to either right or left hand lock. Slipping belts run hotter than they should, and the extra friction wears down the rubber and frays the cords. Generally, a slipping belt or one that is adjusted too tight will be severely glazed along the V-shaped contact area. See Fig. 7-9 for belt wear signs.

Time will eventually destroy even a carefully maintained belt. As the rubber ages, it becomes brittle and cracks. Normal wear begins to take its toll on the rubber and frayed cords will appear along the outside edges of the belt.

Fig. 7-9. Sure signs of a worn belt.

Adjusting Belts

A properly adjusted belt should have between ¼ and ½ inch of play at the center of its longest run. Hold a ruler against the belt as shown in Fig. 7-10. In order to keep that hand steady rest your forearm on some convenient surface such as the top of the radiator. With your free hand depress the belt lightly until it firmly resists the pressure. Adjust the belt as necessary.

In order to adjust the drive belts on most cars, you have to move the driven component closer to or farther away from the drive pulley. Some manufacturers provide an idler pulley along the belt's run, and you can adjust belt tension by moving the pulley closer to (tighten) or farther away from (loosen) the belt.

You adjust the fan/water pump/alternator drive belt by moving the alternator. Locate the alternator pivot and lock bolts as

Fig. 7-10. Hold the ruler steady, depress the belt, and measure the travel.

shown in Fig. 7-11. Loosen each at least two full turns. You want the bolts loose enough to allow you to move the alternator in either direction, but you don't want them so loose that the alternator flops around in its mount.

If you want to tighten the belt, find a suitable pry point, as shown in Fig. 7-12. Never pry against the alternator fins. Pry the alternator away from the drive pulley, as shown in Fig. 7-12. While you hold the alternator in tension, press on the belt at a point in the middle of the top run end eyeball estimate the play. Without releasing the tension on the alternator, tighten the lock

Fig. 7-11. Alternator pivot bolt with wrench on it; lock bolt is to the upper right in the slotted bracket.

Fig. 7-12. Insert your pry bar to give good leverage.

bolt. Remove the pry bar and tighten the pivot bolt. Now, as I previously described in Fig. 7-10, measure the belt free play and correct as necessary.

If you want to loosen the drive belt, loosen the alternator pivot and lock bolts a couple of turns and press down on the top run of the belt. Frequently, a belt that is too tight will pull the alternator toward the drive pulley as soon as you loosen the bolts, and you will have to pry it up to arrive at the correct adjustment.

Power Steering Pump Belt

Locate the pivot and lock bolts, as shown in Fig. 7-13. Loosen each a couple of turns. Many power steering pumps have bosses cast into the body especially for and at a spot convenient for prying. Never pry against the pump body at any point other than the boss provided, because you might break the casting. Follow the adjustment procedure as was described for the alternator belt.

Replacing a Belt

Removing an old belt and installing a new one is as easy as adjusting the belt. Loosen the pivot and lock bolts, swing the component toward the drive pulley as far as it will go, then slip

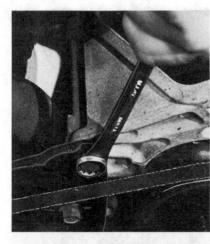

Fig. 7-13. Power-steering pump pivot bolt (wrench) and the lock bolt below it.

Fig. 7-14. Remove the belt from the driven component first.

the belt from the driven component's pulley. See Fig. 7-14. Remove the belt from the remaining pulleys and throw it away. Install the new belt by reversing the removal procedure, and adjust it as described previously.

Remember, any belt that is located behind the alternator belt cannot be removed without first removing the alternator drive belt. Work the belts over one fan blade at a time.

COOLING SYSTEM

Burdened with a variety of belt driven accessories and emission controls, the modern automobile engine demands a lot from its cooling system. Engineers and chemists responded to the demands with pressurized cooling systems and ethylene glycol permanent antifreeze/coolant. Here is how the system works.

The cooling system includes the radiator, fan, water pump, thermostat, water jackets and passages cast into the cylinder block and heads, the heater, and connecting hoses. When you start the engine first thing in the morning, the water pump and fan which are driven off of the same pulley begin working. The fan draws air through the radiator core and circulates it throughout the engine compartment. The water pump circulates coolant through the water jackets of the engine.

During the first several minutes, the thermostat, which is located at the base of the radiator inlet hose and set to open at around 200° F keeps the coolant from entering the radiator core. When the coolant reaches 200° the thermostat opens and allows coolant to flow through the radiator.

The radiator core is made from finned tubes that remove heat from the coolant as it follows a serpentine route from the top of the radiator to the bottom. When the car is at rest, the fan circulates air through the radiator core. Coolant now at a lower temperature enters the water pump through a port on the pump's under side. The pump circulates the coolant through the engine. When you turn the heater on, hot coolant circulates through the heater box as well. Air drawn through the heater core by a small fan circulates through and warms the passenger compartment.

Modern automobile cooling systems are pressurized and, for all practical purposes, sealed. Special radiator caps allow pressure inside the system to reach 12 to 15 pounds per square inch. When the pressure exceeds that limit, a valve in the cap opens and allows some of the hot coolant to escape into a catch tank or out of an overflow tube and onto the ground. As the engine cools, the coolant contracts, and that which flowed into the catch tank returns to the system. Systems without catch tanks simply lose a small amount of coolant every time the radiator cap valve opens. Catch tank systems are sealed in so far as you inspect coolant level and add coolant through the tank cap, and unless you drain and refill or flush the system, you never have to remove the radiator cap. The pressure in the system and the addition of permanent antifreeze which accounts for half of the coolant mixture, raise the boiling point of water to over 260° F.

The word permanent as applied to antifreeze does not mean that it will last indefinitely. It means that the antifreeze should be used year round in all climates, and that it functions as an excellent coolant as well as an antifreeze. Antifreeze also inhibits rust and corrosion throughout the system, and it lubricates the water pump.

Considering those facts, you might want to drain and flush the cooling system of your engine and install fresh antifreeze once every two years. The old antifreeze still protects the system from freezing and boiling over, but its rust and corrosion inhibitors will have been exhausted. Once allowed to accumulate, rust and corrosion deposits can block the system and cause the engine to severely overheat, resulting in expensive damage.

Auto manufacturers fill each new car's cooling system with a 50-50 solution of antifreeze and water at the factory. Making sure that this has actually been done should be part of the dealer's predelivery service, but to be safe, you should probably check it yourself. During the remaining period of time that you own your car, check the coolant level about as often as you check the engine's oil level and test for specific gravity at least once a year. If you live in an area of the country where the winters are cold, test the system in the fall. If you live in a more temperate climate, test it anytime.

Checking Coolant Level

The overflow catch tanks used in some auto cooling systems are usually made from a translucent plastic that shows the coolant level. The tank will be marked with a cold minimum and a hot minimum level line. Simply look at the tank to check the coolant level of the engine. Always add coolant to the system by pouring it into the overflow tank, and it makes no difference whether the engine is hot or cold.

In order to see how much coolant is in a system without an overflow tank, remove the radiator cap and peer into the top of the radiator. Always check the coolant level when this type of system is cool. The coolant should be an inch and a half or so below the base of the filler neck.

There are times, however, when you will have to check the coolant level of a hot system, in which case you must be very careful. All modern cooling systems are pressurized, and there are three different types of radiator caps and methods for releasing the pressure before you remove the cap. Many of these caps will have instructions printed on the top. Read these first.

On some radiator caps, you will find a button to push or a lever to pull up that opens a valve in the cap and releases the pressure. Using a cloth or a household hot pad, push the button or lift the lever and hold it until the whooshing stops. Now using the same cloth to protect your hand, turn the cap counterclockwise until the ears on the cap line up with the slots on the lip of the filler neck. Remove the cap.

Fig. 7-15. One example of a pressurized radiator cap.

If the pressure cap has no button or lever (Fig. 7-15), place the cloth over the cap, then turn the cap counterclockwise about ¼ turn until it stops. Do not push down on the cap. Remove your hand and let the pressure escape. When the whooshing stops, press down on the cap and turn it counterclockwise until the cap ears line up with the filler neck slots. Remove the cap. Always be careful when you remove the cap from a hot radiator. Remember that the coolant temperature can reach 260° F, and it will cause severe burns. If you have to add liquid to a hot system, do it only while the engine is running.

If you have to add coolant to your car's cooling system several times a year, it might be a good idea to mix a gallon, half antifreeze and half water, and carry it in your trunk or keep it in the garage. If you add only water every time the system needs topping up, you will dilute the coolant and reduce both freeze and boil-over protection. Some service people recommend that you add pure antifreeze to the system every time it needs topping up, but one fact that you should remember if you choose to follow their advice . . . pure antifreeze freezes at a higher temperature than does the 50-50 mixture. Whichever you choose, it's a good idea to test the freeze protection of the system at least once a year.

Specific Gravity Test

The specific gravity of the coolant indicates the level of freeze protection provided. The hydrometer used for this test will usually show the specific gravity in number values as well as in degrees Fahrenheit.

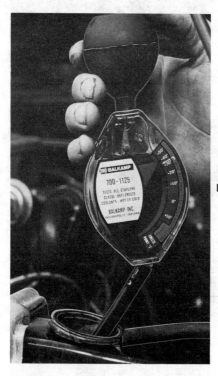

Fig. 7-16. Reading the hydrometer.

Before performing the test, run the engine until the radiator top is hot to the touch. You can be fairly sure at this point that the coolant is sufficiently homogenized. Remove the radiator cap according to the instructions given previously. Dip your hydrometer into the coolant, squeeze the bulb, and release it slowly. Read the hydrometer at eye level as shown in Fig. 7-16. Squeeze the coolant back into the radiator and replace the cap. Rinse the hydrometer in clear running water. That will prevent antifreeze residue from causing the float to stick during subsequent tests. If the test showed inadequate freeze protection, add antifreeze, run the engine for several minutes, and test again.

If the system is full, but it doesn't have adequate freeze protection, you will have to drain some of the coolant from the radiator. You will find a drain petcock on the bottom or bottom front of the radiator, as shown in Fig. 7-17. Before opening the drain, release the pressure of the system and remove the cap. Loosen the petcock with a pliers and drain off about a quart of coolant into a bucket. Top off the radiator with antifreeze after you have closed the drain petcock, replace the cap, run the engine for a few minutes, then test the specific gravity again. If your car radiator doesn't have a drain petcock, you will have to remove the radiator outlet hose at the bottom. Unscrew the hose clamp, slide it out of your way, and twist the hose from the fitting.

Fig. 7-17. Locate the radiator drain petcock.

In order for the radiator to remove heat from the coolant, air has to circulate around the finned coils. Located just behind the grill, the radiator collects bugs, paper scraps, and all manner of flying debris. Over a period of years, the collection of debris may become thick enough to substantially reduce the air flow and impair the radiator's cooling efficiency. Clean the radiator once a year by placing a garden hose behind it and spraying a high pressure stream of water through it.

Every time that you check the coolant level, examine the rubber seal on the bottom of the radiator cap for cracks, tears, or pinched spots that might cause a pressure leak. Examine the valve spring for heavy corrosion. Once a year or so, you might want to have the system pressure tested by a competent professional.

Antifreeze manufacturers recommend that you drain and flush the cooling system once every two years. With the help of a

Fig. 7-18. Typical cooling system flushing kit and flushing agent.

flushing kit like the one shown in Fig. 7-18, the job is more time consuming than difficult. Before you buy a kit, measure the inside diameter of the heater hose that runs from the engine heater box. See Fig. 7-19.

Flushing the Cooling System

First remove the radiator cap then open the drain petcock. Let the radiator drain while you install the flushing tee in the heater hose. Choose a convenient spot along the hose length and cut through it with a utility knife. Place a hose clamp from the kit over each end of the hose and install the flushing tee, as

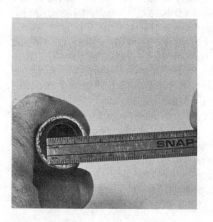

Fig. 7-19. Measuring the inside diameter of the radiator hose.

shown in Fig. 7-20. Tighten the clamps until the outside diameter begins to compress.

After all of the coolant has drained from the radiator, close the drain petcock. If your car has a cross flow radiator (characterized by the filler cap at one or the other top corner of the radiator . . . check specifications in the owner's manual) leave the drain petcock open. Place the splash tube in the filler neck. Uncap the flushing tee and attach the garden hose to it.

Adjust the car heater to "High" then turn on the water supply to the garden hose. The heater controls on many newer cars and on those equipped with air conditioning are vacuum operated. If your car is so equipped, start the engine and let it idle until the flushing is completed. Continue flushing until the water coming out of the splash tube is clean.

Fig. 7-20. Installing the flushing tee.

Shut off the water, disconnect the hose from the flushing tee, and drain the radiator. Close the drain petcock and fill the radiator with clear water. At this point, you might want to add a flushing agent to the system, especially if your car is several years old and the cooling system has been neglected. Replace the radiator cap. Run the engine until the top of the radiator is hot to the touch, then drain it. If you have used a flushing agent, repeat the flushing procedure after the cooling system has cooled.

After the radiator has finished draining, close the petcock and let the system cool. Consult your owner's manual for cooling system capacity. If for example, your car has a 16-quart system, add 8 quarts of antifreeze to the cool radiator. Put the cap on and run the engine until the top of the radiator is hot. Remove the cap and check the coolant level. Add water until the coolant level is within 1½ inches of the bottom of the filler neck. Replace the cap, run the engine for several minutes, then test the system for specific gravity.

Replacing Worn Hoses and Tired Thermostats

Time and a harsh environment cause cooling system hoses to crack, split, and become spongy. In many cases when a hose reaches this stage of deterioration, it will cave in or buckle at the bends.

The hose may be secured to the fitting with a screw type or a spring type hose clamp. Turn the screw counterclockwise until the hose clamp is loose enough to slip out of your way. Pinch the ears of the spring clamp together with a pliers and slide the clamp away from the fitting. With a utility knife, cut the hose along the fitting and peel it off. Repeat the procedure on the other fitting. Take the old hose with you when you go to buy a new one. Be sure to give the counter sales person the make, model, year, engine type and size, and the location of the hose. See Fig. 7-21 for hose identification. The top, large diameter hose

Fig. 7-21. Cooling system hoses.

carries coolant from the engine to the radiator. The small diameter hose on the left carries coolant from the block to the heater. The hose next to it carries coolant from the heater to the water pump.

Clean the hose fitting with a wire brush. Lubricate the end of the hose with a solution of liquid detergent and water mixed at a couple of drops in 8 ounces of water. Twist the new hose onto one fitting. Slip the hose clamps onto the hose, then push the free end of the hose onto the other fitting. Tighten the hose clamps. When you change the top radiator hose, drain about a gallon of coolant from the radiator. Before you change the bottom hose, empty the radiator.

After you have finished installing the new hose, add the necessary amount of 50-50 coolant to the system, start the engine, and let it run for several minutes. Examine your connections for leaks.

Thermostat

The thermostat is a heat sensitive valve that prevents coolant from entering the radiator until it reaches a prescribed temperature. Without the thermostat, warmups would take longer, the engine would run too cool and lose some of its combustion efficiency. That's what happens when the thermostat sticks open. You would hardly notice the difference in the summer, but in winter, the water temperature gauge would stay glued to the cold peg, and the heater would provide only a suggestion of heat. If the thermostat sticks closed, the engine will overheat and stall after a short time. Cooling system rust and corrosion cause the thermostat to fail.

Fig. 7-22. Removing the thermostat housing bolts.

The thermostat is located in a housing atop the engine near the water pump at the beginning of the hose that carries coolant to the radiator. Before you open the housing, drain about a gallon of coolant from the radiator into a clean bucket. With your ratchet, medium length extension, and appropriate socket, remove the housing mounting nuts or bolts, as shown in Fig. 7-22.

Fig. 7-23. The thermostat fits into the housing spring down.

Lift the cover up and bend it out of your way. It might be stuck to the gasket, in which case some prudent tapping with a plastic mallet should loosen it. Note the way the thermostat sits in the passage. See Fig. 7-23. Remove the thermostat and take it with you when you go out to buy a new one.

Scrape the old gasket material from both surfaces. Place the new thermostat into the housing, install the new gasket, and bolt the cover into place. You might want to coat both sides of the new gasket with a nonhardening gasket cement. Pour the coolant from your drain bucket back into the radiator, replace the cap, and run the engine while you check for leaks around the thermostat housing cover. Be sure to stay clear of the fan. After a few minutes, check the coolant level and top up as necessary.

CHAPTER 8

Engine, Transmission, and Differential Lubrication

Old-timers will tell you that clean oil is the key, the single most important ingredient, to long engine life. I say old-timers, because the latest trends regarding oil change intervals and the latest technology regarding the lasting qualities of oil additives suggest that you change oil and filter every 6 to 15 thousand miles. If you use one of the synthetic oils and follow the company's advice, you can drive for one year or up to 24 thousand miles on one oil change.

Times have changed, and it is a safe bet that these folks, especially the automobile manufacturers, aren't leading you astray. On the other hand, oil and filters are cheaper than new engines. I'm old fashioned when it comes to oil and filter changes. During the warm season, I change both as soon as the engine consumes a half quart or so. Depending upon the make, the engine type, and your driving habits, a car might run for a few thousand miles before the engine uses a noticeable amount of oil. In my experience, as the miles piled up and the oil became more contaminated, the engine used more of it. I have seen this happen with a variety of cars where oil consumption began at 1 to 3 thousand miles and increased as the mileage increased. During the cold months, I change oil and filter once every month.

The subject of oil brands, change intervals, and additives is at least controversial among enthusiasts and sometimes religious. If you find yourself in a flap about oil and filter change intervals and brand claims, remember that you cannot go wrong if you follow the auto maker's recommendations.

CHANGING ENGINE OIL

The engine oil sump is located at the very bottom of the engine block. It is a sheet metal reservoir that is secured to the block with bolts placed a few inches apart all around the perimeter and sealed against leaks with a gasket. A drain plug screwed into the sump (Fig. 8-1) allows you or a mechanic to drain the oil.

A pump circulates oil throughout the engine, and when it reaches the valve gear at the top of the cylinder head, it simply drains back down into the sump. Bear this fact in mind when you are checking the oil level. Allow a minute or two after you have shut the engine off for the oil in the heads to drain into the sump. If you check the oil immediately after shutting the engine off, the dipstick will read low.

Always change the oil when the engine is hot. Hot oil flows more easily. Sludge in the bottom of the sump will be softer and more of it will flow out with the oil, and it will take less time for the oil to drain.

Move your car onto a level place, shut the engine off, and wait a couple of minutes to allow oil in the upper part of the engine to drain down into the sump. Set the parking brake and make sure

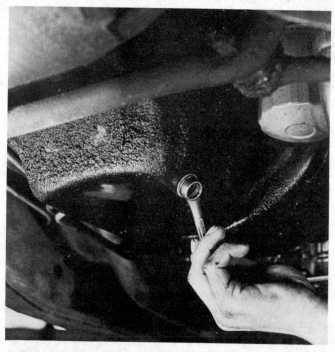

Fig. 8-1. Engine oil sump drain plug located in the lower section of the sump.

that the transmission is in "Park" (automatic transmission) or in gear (manual transmission). Here is where you can save some time and effort.

Normally, the next step would be jacking the car up and securing it with jack stands. In order to keep the car level, you have to place all four jack stands. Don't bother. The engine is placed over the front wheels, and the sump drain plug is usually only a little more than an arm's reach from the bumper. Most cars are built high enough so that you can slip right under there with little or no effort.

Find something to lie on such as a drop cloth or a large piece of cardboard. Place it under the car. Slide your drain pan, large enough to hold six quarts, under the drain plug. Take the appropriate wrench, usually a 9/16 inch, and slither under the car. Loosen the drain plug by turning it counterclockwise. Finish unscrewing the plug with your hand. The drain plug will be hot, so you might need a cloth to protect your fingers from burns. Let the oil drain until only a very slow drip flow remains. Replace the drain plug, and add fresh oil.

What brand of oil you use in your car's engine hardly matters as long as the quality of that oil meets or exceeds the auto maker's specifications. How will you know? Read the owner's manual then read the specifications on the can. You will find printed and/or embossed on the top of the can information about the viscosity range and more important, the service rating.

Viscosity range is expressed, "SAE 10W-40" for multigrades and means that the oil acts like a straight 10W oil when it is cold, and acts like a straight 40W when it is hot. "HD" means heavy duty. The service rating is expressed in the letters SE, SD, SC, SB, and SA. These letters indicate the quality of the protection that the oil offers against wear, rust, high temperatures, corrosion, etc. SE rated oil is the highest quality, and it is recommended by auto makers for all cars built since 1972.

SD rated oil was designed for cars built between 1968 and 1972 . . . the beginning of emission controls. SC rated oil was developed for cars built during the sixties through 1967. If you are interested in long engine life and at the same time extending the period between changes, you had better use SE rated oil. If you choose to change the oil and filter every 1500 to 2000 miles, you will probably find SD rated oil fine for even late model cars and SC rated oil adequate for pre-1972 models. As long as your car is protected by the manufacturer's warranty, you have to use SE rated oil.

Before you add fresh oil, consult the owner's manual for information regarding oil sump capacity. Most American cars require 3 to 5 quarts without a filter change and a full quart more

Fig. 8-2. Locate and remove the oil filler cap.

with a filter change. Locate the filler cap as shown in Fig. 8-2, and remove it. Insert the oil can pour spout into the can as shown in Fig. 8-3 and add the first quart. Wipe up any spills with a cloth.

CHANGING THE OIL FILTER

The oil filter on modern American cars is a cylinder-shaped canister. It screws onto a fitting that is bolted to the side of the engine block. The filter's exact location varies according to the

Fig. 8-3. Place the opening blade of the pour spout close to the rim of the can and push down firmly.

auto maker and the type of engine. You will find the filter high on the left (driver's) side of in-line 4 and 6 cylinder engines as shown in Fig. 8-4. You can reach it from above. You will find the filter low, very near the oil sump, usually on the left side of V6 and V8 engines. You will have to raise the car and crawl under it in order to change the filter. See Fig. 8-5.

Locate the filter. Jack the car up if you have to and secure it with jack stands. Place a drain pan under the filter. Self-contained, disposable, screw-on filters should always be tightened by hand,

Fig. 8-4. Location of oil filter on in-line 4 and 6 cylinder engines.

and you should be able to loosen them by hand as well. If your filter proves stubborn, use an oil filter wrench, as shown in Fig. 8-6. Position the wrench on the filter so that the counterclockwise rotation tightens the wrench strap on the filter body. After you have loosened the filter finish removing it by hand.

Before you install the new filter, wipe the fitting with a clean, lint-free cloth. Spread a thin coating of clean oil on the rubber sealing gasket of the new filter and screw it onto the fitting. *Do not cross thread the filter*. Tighten the filter one-half to one full turn after the gasket has seated. Presuming that you are changing the oil and filter at the same time, add fresh engine oil, start the

Fig. 8-5. Location of the oil filter on V6 and V8 engines.

engine, and check for leaks around the filter. When you buy a new filter, always state the make, year, model, and engine type and size (cubic inch displacement generally found under "specifications" in the owner's manual). Be sure the filter that you buy is made for your car's engine.

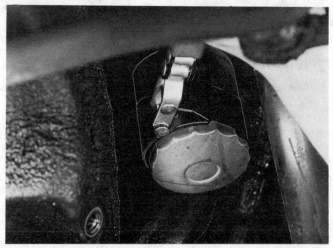

Fig. 8-6. Loosen stubborn filters with an oil filter wrench.

Routine engine oil level checks should be done every five hundred to one thousand miles. Locate the dipstick as shown in Fig. 8-7. Pull it out and wipe the oil from it with a clean cloth. Reinsert the dipstick, pull it out, and read the level as shown in Fig. 8-8. If the oil is at the "add" line, the engine needs one quart. Any level between the "add" and "full" lines is okay, but be sure to check the level again in another 500 miles. If you add oil at home, you can add less than a quart to top up the sump. Cover open oil cans with one of the plastic covers that comes with one pound coffee cans.

Fig. 8-7. Location of the engine oil dipstick.

AUTOMATIC TRANSMISSION OIL

The oil in your automatic transmission both lubricates the gears and acts as the hydraulic fluid for shifting. A dipstick that looks like the engine oil sump dipstick is provided for checking the fluid level. It is located at the rear of the engine (Fig. 8-9), and it is usually twice as long as the engine dipstick.

Check transmission fluid level only after it has reached operating temperature. That requires 15 to 20 miles of highway driving. Checking the level of cold fluid will give you a low reading which

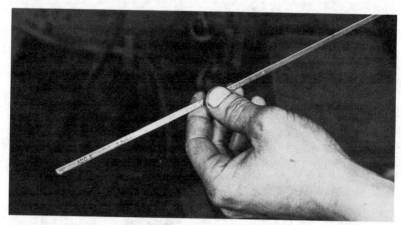

Fig. 8-8. Reading the oil level.

tends to make people overfill the transmission. Overfilling causes the oil to foam, and it increases the pressure within the transmission case which can blow out seals and gaskets.

Clean the area around the top of the dipstick before you remove it. Even the smallest particle of dirt in the transmission's intricate passages can cause trouble. Remove the dipstick, wipe

Fig. 8-9. Location of automatic transmission oil level dipstick.

it off with a clean lint-free cloth, reinsert it, pull it out, and read the level. Any level between "add" and "full" is adequate. If you have to add fluid, consult the owner's manual for the correct type. Insert a small funnel in the dipstick tower and add oil. Add a little at a time and recheck the level each time to make sure that you do not overfill the transmission.

Like engine oil, automatic transmission fluid becomes contaminated, and you should change it about every 25,000 miles. You will need a ratchet, short extension, the appropriate socket, gasket scraper, a drain pan of more than 3 gallons capacity, a parts washing pan and brush, oil pan filter/gasket kit for your car, and enough of the right fluid for your car. Ford transmissions need about 12 quarts, General Motors cars about 3 quarts, and Chrysler 8.5 to 9 quarts.

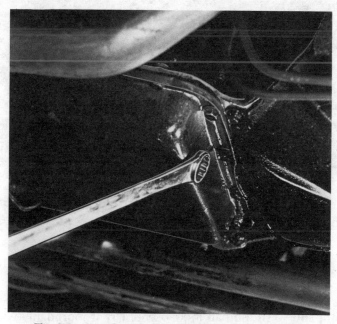

Fig. 8-10. Location of automatic transmission oil pan.
This one has a drain plug.

Drive the car for a few miles to warm up the fluid. Jack up both ends of the car and support it with four jack stands. Try to keep the car level. The sheet metal transmission cover is bolted to the underside of the transmission case. See Fig. 8-10. You will find a drain plug in the transmission oil pan of some early model cars. Simply remove that to drain the oil. Refer to pan removal

113

instructions that follow for removing and cleaning the pan and screen or replacing the filter.

In order to drain the oil from late model automatic transmissions, you have to remove the oil pan. Place your drain pan under the transmission. Remove all of the pan bolts except for those along the front of the pan. After you have removed the bolts, support the pan with your hand, and loosen the bolts holding the front of the pan (Fig. 8-11). Lower the rear of the pan and let the oil drain into the drain pan. Use a putty knife or thin bladed screwdriver to break a sticking oil pan free of the gasket. After the oil has drained, remove the remaining bolts.

Fig. 8-11. Support the pan with your hand and let the oil drain from the rear of the pan.

Remove the transmission oil pan, scrape any of the old gasket from it, and wash the pan in kerosene. Dry it thoroughly with a clean, lint-free cloth and set it aside. Scrape the old gasket material from the transmission case, as shown in Fig. 8-12.

Remove the oil filter or strainer assembly. It may simply clip into place or be screwed to the case. Fig. 8-13 shows one example. Some transmissions have reusable wire filter screens. Clean these thoroughly, and dry with a clean lint-free cloth before reinstalling. Remove the disposable filter, install a new gasket as shown in Fig. 8-14, and install a new filter. Coat it with transmission oil to get it to stick to the surface of the case. You will find a long neck

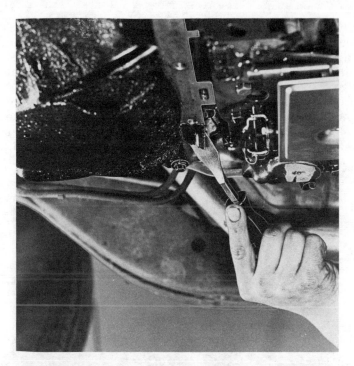

Fig. 8-12. Scrape the old gasket material from the transmission case.

Fig. 8-13. Removing one type of automatic transmission oil filter.

on the filter in General Motors Turbo Hydra-Matic transmissions. When you remove the filter, you should find an O-ring located at the bulge of the neck. Make sure that this O-ring comes out with the filter, and make sure that you install a new one at the bulge.

Coat the gasket surface of the clean oil pan with a thin film of nonhardening gasket cement, as shown in Fig. 8-15. Place the new gasket on the pan and line up the bolt holes. Clean the mounting bolts. Make sure that the pan is free of lint, dust, and dirt, then hold it up against the transmission case. Install the

Fig. 8-14. Replace the filter gasket located under the filter with a new gasket.

bolts and tighten each one as far as you can with your fingers. Finish tightening in a criss-cross pattern. If you have a torque wrench, tighten the pan bolts to 10 or 12 foot-pounds. Do not overtighten the bolts.

Add the prescribed amount of oil. See checking fluid level described earlier in this chapter. With the gear selector in "Park" and the parking brake on, start the car and let it idle. After the engine warms up a little, shift the transmission through all of the gears and return the selector to "Park." Shut the engine off and check the fluid level. It should be about ¼ inch below the "add" line. Lower the car and drive it until the transmission

Fig. 8-15. Coat the oil pan gasket surface with a thin film
of nonhardening gasket cement.

reaches operating temperature. When you check the level at operating temperature, the dipstick should read "Full."

MANUAL TRANSMISSIONS

Manual shift transmissions rarely need an oil change, but maintaining the proper level is important. You will find the drain plug located on the bottom of the case, and the filler plug on the side. See Fig. 8-16. Usually the gear oil level should be at or about ½ inch below the filler plug threads. Oil will seep out of the filler plug when you remove it, or you should be able to feel the oil by inserting your little finger into the hole. Standard transmissions require 80/90W Hypoy gear lube unless otherwise specified by the manufacturer.

Always drain the oil from a warm transmission. Jack up the car and support it with four jack stands. Place the drain plug pan under the transmission and remove the drain plug. Allow about five minutes of drain time. Replace the plug. These are usually tapered pipe thread and need no gasket. Remove the filler plug. Fill an oil syringe with gear lube and inject it into the transmission. Fill until the oil begins to flow out of the filler hole. Wait until the flow stops, then install the filler plug. If you don't have an oil syringe, fill a large oil squirt can and pump the oil into the case.

117

DIFFERENTIAL OIL

Like manual transmissions, modern car differentials don't really need an oil change. The differential is the large bulge in the center of the rear axle housing. Check the oil level by removing the filler plug on the differential cover plate. See Fig. 8-17. The

Fig. 8-16. Manual transmission filler plug. Drain plug is bolt indicated by finger.

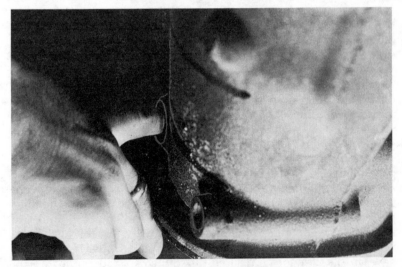

Fig. 8-17. Check the oil level by removing the filler plug and inserting your little finger.

oil should be at or ½ inch below the filler plug threads. Use your little finger for a dipstick.

In order to drain and replace the oil, you have to remove the differential cover plate. You will need a new gasket. Drain the oil from a warm housing. Remove the cover plate bolts. Let the oil drain for about five minutes. Scrape remnants of the old gasket from the differential housing and from the cover plate. Wash the cover plate in kerosene and wipe it dry with a clean cloth. Spread a thin coat of nonhardening gasket cement on the cover plate gasket surface, and press the new gasket into place. Install the cover plate. Tighten the bolts by hand then finish the job with your socket in a criss-cross pattern. Fill your syringe, and inject the oil into the differential filler hole. Use only 80/90 Hypoy gear lube or the auto maker's recommended oil. Replace the filler plug, drive the car a short distance and check the cover for leaks around the gasket.

CHAPTER 9

What Makes the Engine Run?

Just when the doomsayers are muttering last rites over the internal combustion, reciprocating piston engine, engineers find a way to clean up exhaust emissions, improve fuel economy, and increase horsepower. Once we realize that these engines will run on a variety of fuels with little change from current design, we can expect to see them around for another 80-odd years.

The internal combustion engine inhales fuel and air, burns it, and exhales the spent gases. The products of this respiration are horsepower and torque. Horsepower is, to quote Webster, "a standard unit of power equal in the U.S. to 746 watts." A meaningless definition to most of us, but we do know that large amounts of horsepower allow the car to accelerate faster and reach higher speeds.

Torque, on the other hand, is the amount of twisting force measured in foot-pounds that the engine develops at the crankshaft. Torque and horsepower spread over a broad range of engine speeds in revolutions per minute and transferred through a series of gears and shafts to the rear or front wheels make your car driveable.

The major components of the engine starting at the bottom are the crankcase, cylinder block, and cylinder head(s). Housed within are the crankshaft, connecting rods, pistons and rings, piston pins, camshaft, tappets, pushrods, rocker arms, valves, valve return springs, assorted bearings, and a host of miscellaneous parts that help tie everything together.

Gears or chain and sprockets tie the crankshaft and the camshaft together so that one cannot rotate without rotating the other. An oil pump, usually geared to the camshaft, circulates oil through passages cast into the block and heads to the moving parts. A variety of seals and gaskets keep the oil and coolant in and the air out.

In some detail now, here is what goes on inside and outside the engine. When you turn the ignition key to "start," you complete an electrical circuit from the battery to the engine's starter motor. A gear on the starter motor shaft engages gear teeth cut into the outside edge of the engine flywheel. The flywheel is bolted to the rear end of the crankshaft. As seen from the driver's seat, the starter motor rotates clockwise, and in turn, rotates the engine counterclockwise at about 200 revolutions per minute.

Fig. 9-1. Camshaft throw at left of cutout; cam and tappets at the top; connecting rod in the center.

Connecting rods attached to crankshaft throws, which are eccentric with the center line of the crankshaft, move the pistons up and down in the cylinder bores. See Fig. 9-1. A small sprocket pressed onto and keyed to the crankshaft drives the timing chain which, in turn, drives a larger sprocket pressed onto and keyed to the camshaft. As the crankshaft rotates so does the cam, but at a lower speed.

Cast into the camshaft are a series of lobes or eccentric peaks machined in such a way that they are rounded at the top and at each corner of their triangular shape. The entire lobe surface is machined to a shiny smoothness. The lobes act upon tappets, or cam followers as they are sometimes called, that are guided by tubes cast into the block. As the cam rotates, the tappets move up and down with the rise and fall of the cam lobe peaks. Pushrods resting in hemispherical indentations on the top of the tappets extend upwards to the valve rocker arms where they are located by another indentation in the end of the rocker arm. See Fig. 9-2.

The rocker arm pivots on a shaft that is bolted to the cylinder head. As the cam lobe reaches its peak, it raises the tappet and pushrod. The pushrod forces the rocker arm to pivot like a seesaw. The end of the rocker arm opposite the pushrod acts upon a valve that moves down and up in a guide that is concentric with the valve stem and return springs. See Fig. 9-3. When

Fig. 9-2. Valve gear—pushrods, rocker arms, and springs.

the cam lobe returns to its lowest point, the tappet, pushrod, and rocker arm retreat from the valve, and the return spring which is keyed to the valve stem closes the valve. There are usually two valves for each cylinder. One of them opens and closes the intake port, and the other one opens and closes the exhaust port.

The ports are passages cast into the cylinder head. One end of the inlet port opens to the carburetor and atmospheric pressure, and the other end opens into the combustion chamber. One end of the exhaust opens to the combustion chamber, and the

Fig. 9-3. Valves and springs.

other end opens to the exhaust manifold. The valve uncovers and covers the port as though it were a manhole cover opened and closed from street level by a post attached to its center. The stem side of the valve head is bevelled and seats on a combustion chamber surface that is machined to match. The two surfaces, under ideal conditions, form a perfect leakproof seal. See Fig. 9-4.

A gear machined into the camshaft and one machined into the distributor shaft mesh and translate the horizontal rotation of the cam into the distributor's vertical rotation. The gears are precisely timed so that the distributor will deliver the spark to the correct cylinder at the correct time.

Regardless of the number of cylinders contained within the engine block, cylinder number one always fires first. The order in which the remaining cylinders fire varies with engine design and the designer's preference. General Motors V8 engines fire 1-8-4-3-6-5-7-2. To simplify matters a bit, let's forget about the other 7 cylinders and just follow number one through its 4 cycles.

Let's assume that piston number one was at the highest point of its stroke (top dead center) and about to begin the intake stroke when you engaged the starter motor. The events that lead to a running engine occur very rapidly, within a few seconds if the engine is well tuned. Therefore, we have to visualize these events in slow motion if we hope to understand them. The starter motor begins to rotate the crankshaft. Crankshaft throw and connecting rod number one pull the piston down. At the same time, the camshaft rotates, and the lobe beneath the number one intake valve

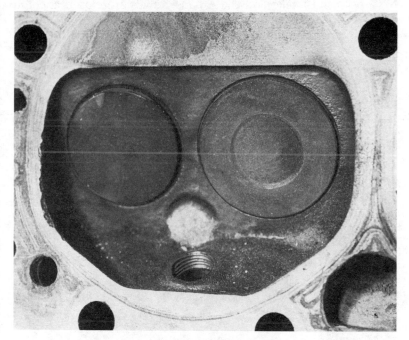

Fig. 9-4. Combustion chamber—exhaust valve head at left, intake valve head at right.

tappet begins to raise the tappet, pushrod, and one end of the rocker arm. The rocker arm pivots and begins opening the valve. A few more degrees of crankshaft and camshaft rotation opens the intake valve all the way. See Fig. 9-5.

Rings resting in grooves cut into the outside circumference of the piston near the top press against the cylinder wall and form a seal. As the piston descends, it creates a partial vacuum in the cylinder. Once the intake valve begins to open, cylinder number one is vented to the atmosphere through the intake port and the carburetor. Atmospheric pressure rushes through the carburetor throat to fill the vacuum created by the piston's descent. As the air passes through the carburetor, the relatively small throat area accelerates the flow. The speeding air creates a low pressure in the throat that draws gasoline from a reservoir in the carburetor and injects it into the air stream. The air stream atomizes the fuel, and the mixture enters the combustion chamber.

A few more degrees of crankshaft rotation brings the piston to the bottom of its stroke (bottom dead center). Shortly after the piston reaches bottom dead center, the camshaft has rotated far enough to allow the valve spring to close the intake valve. Now both the intake and the exhaust valves are closed and the cylinder is sealed against any influence from the atmosphere. The crankshaft continues to rotate and forces the piston back up

Fig. 9-5. Intake stroke—intake valve open all the way.

toward the cylinder head. See Fig. 9-6. This is called the compression stroke. Compressing the gaseous mixture of fuel and air into the confines of the combustion chamber raises the mixture's temperature and promotes more efficient burning.

In the meantime, the distributor shaft and the breaker point cam which are geared to the camshaft have been rotating. At a specified number of degrees of crankshaft rotation before the piston reaches top dead center, the breaker point cam opens the points and discharges a spark across the spark plug's electrode gap.

The spark ignites the fuel/air mixture. The mixture does not explode, but it does burn very, very rapidly. Burning changes the fuel/air mixture to a variety of gases that expand with enormous force and drive the piston downward. This is called the power stroke. See Fig. 9-6. At this stage of the game, the engine should continue to run without the starter motor's help.

At a specified point in degrees of crankshaft rotation after the piston reaches bottom dead center, a lobe on the camshaft engages the exhaust tappet, pushrod, rocker arm, and valve, opens the valve and allows the rapidly rising piston to push the burned gases from the cylinder into the exhaust port and exhaust manifold. See Fig. 9-7. At a specific number of degrees of crankshaft

Fig. 9-6. Compression and power strokes—both valves tightly closed.

and camshaft rotation after the piston reaches top dead center of the exhaust stroke, the exhaust valve closes and the intake valve begins to open. The entire cycle begins again.

The crankshaft throws are arranged in a way that permits each of the 4, 6, or 8 cylinders to begin their four stroke cycles at times relative to one another that will keep the engine running. All of the moving parts vital to the completion of these cycles are geared together or timed so that the cycles are orchestrated into one continuous flow of smooth power.

FUEL SYSTEM

Your car's fuel system includes the gas tank and cap, the fuel lines, fuel pump, fuel filter, and the carburetor. A variety of emission control devices associated with the fuel system might be included here as well, but except for the charcoal canister which I will discuss later, these devices do not affect the system's basic concepts or fit in with the book's basic nature.

You will find the gas tank on most cars mounted to the chassis beneath the trunk floor. A tubular steel fuel line carries gasoline to the engine mounted fuel pump. A float in the tank is electrically connected to the fuel gauge on the instrument panel. The float and gauge work together to monitor the tank's fuel level and display it on the fuel gauge.

Most cars are equipped with mechanical diaphragm fuel pumps that are driven by a lobe on the camshaft or distributor shaft. The lobe acts on a pushrod or rocker arm and linkage to move

Fig. 9-7. Exhaust stroke—exhaust valve open all the way.

the diaphragm in and out. The inlet stroke creates a vacuum which draws fuel from the tank, and the output stroke creates pressure which forces the fuel through a line to the carburetor. A check valve in the intake side prevents fuel from escaping back into the feed line. A filter located in the line somewhere between the outlet port and the carburetor removes any debris that might be suspended in the fuel.

Some cars are equipped with electric fuel pumps which are usually mounted near the gas tank. A tiny electric motor drives a high speed impeller that draws fuel from the tank, through the pump, and out into the line to the carburetor.

CARBURETOR

The carburetor is a device designed to provide your car's engine with the correct mixture of fuel and air over a wide range of engine speeds from idle to the maximum safe limit. Fuel from the pump enters the carburetor float bowl via a needle valve. See Fig. 9-8. As the fuel level in the float rises, it raises the float which eventually pushes the needle into its seat and stops the fuel flow.

Fig. 9-8. Carburetor float. The needle and seat are located above the pivot arm.

As the fuel in the float bowl is used, the float sinks. Fuel line pressure opens the needle valve and allows more fuel to flow into the float bowl. In actual practice, the level of fuel in the float bowl remains fairly constant, and as long as the engine demands fuel, the float rarely has a chance to completely shut off the flow. The float chamber is vented to the atmosphere.

The carburetor works on the principle of negative pressure or partial vacuum. You remember that the intake stroke of the engine creates a partial vacuum in the cylinder. Well, this vacuum is felt throughout the intake system. Atmospheric pressure rushes to fill the void. This rush of air through the carburetor throat is controlled by butterfly valves which resemble pivoting trapdoors. See Fig. 9-9. A venturi in the carburetor throat, the cross section of which looks like back to back parentheses)(, accelerates the air flow even more and creates an area of very low pressure. See Fig. 9-10. Note the idle air bleed holes just beneath the screws at the top of the picture.

Atmospheric pressure acting on the fuel in the float bowl works in concert with the low pressure in the carburetor throat and forces fuel into the air flow via a metering jet. See Fig. 9-11. At idle when the butterfly valve is closed and air flow through the venturi is severely limited, there is not enough vacuum in

Fig. 9-9. Throttle butterfly valves open. Note the main fuel nozzles sticking out from the throat walls.

the venturi to draw fuel through the main fuel nozzle. In this instance, the fuel/air mixture is controlled by the idle/low speed circuit.

The circuit consists of the following: the idle delivery tube that transports fuel from the float bowl to the carburetor throat; the idle air bleed which is a tiny passageway that opens to the atmosphere high in the throat near the top of the venturi on the float bowl side; the idle port which is a tiny hole drilled into the throat wall just below the closed butterfly; a tapered screw that seats into the idle port and can be adjusted to vary the amount

Fig. 9-10. Carburetor venturi.

Fig. 9-11. Main metering jets. The large jet in the center is the power circuit jet.

of fuel flowing through the idle port; and two off-idle ports drilled into the throat wall just above the closed butterfly valve.

At idle when the butterfly valve is closed, manifold vacuum is high. Atmospheric pressure acting on the fuel in the float bowl works together with the manifold vacuum to draw fuel through the idle tube and into the air bleed passage. The fuel/air mixture created in the air bleed passage passes over the tapered idle screw, which regulates the flow by its position in the port, and enters the carburetor throat just below the butterfly valve. See Fig. 9-12.

Fig. 9-12. Idle ports and off idle ports indicated by the mechanic's thumb.

When you depress the throttle pedal only slightly, the butterfly valve opens far enough so that it is above the off-idle ports. The increased air flow creates low pressure at the off-idle ports which draws fuel through the ports and into the carburetor throat. The off-idle ports enrich the mixture to compensate for the increased air flow and provide a smooth transition from idle to just above idle.

Opening the throttle or butterfly valves farther increases the air flow enough to create sufficient vacuum in the venturi to draw fuel from the main fuel nozzle. This high speed/partial load circuit provides the engine with the correct fuel/air ratio from part to full throttle.

Fig. 9-13. Accelerator pump. Plunger near center of
float controls power circuit needle.

The "full power" circuit actually serves two purposes—it improves fuel economy at part throttle and increases the fuel flow demanded by a wide open throttle. A tapered or two-step metering rod is raised and lowered in the main jet by a linkage connected to the throttle linkage or by a spring loaded plunger and manifold vacuum. At part throttle, the larger diameter portion of the rod meters the fuel and maintains the correct mixture.

When the driver pushes the accelerator pedal to the floor and opens the butterfly valve all the way, air flow increases. At the same time, the metering rod linkage lifts the rod high enough so that the smaller diameter portion of the rod is in the main jet. The fuel flow increases to maintain the correct fuel/air mixture. A spring on the vacuum-operated metering rod raises the rod when the wide open throttle reduces intake manifold vacuum.

The accelerator pump is a small diaphragm pump that is connected to the throttle through a linkage. Other circuits of the carburetor cannot respond quickly enough to maintain the correct fuel/air mixture during the first moment after the butterfly valve opens. When you depress the accelerator pedal, the pump squirts an extra supply of fuel to the air stream to enrich the mixture. The squirt is a short duration one that allows the carburetor's main circuit time to catch up to the increased air flow. The accelerator pump eliminates the hesitation normally associated with a too lean fuel/air mixture. See Fig. 9-13.

Cold starts demand more fuel than the low speed and idle circuits can supply. Instead of increasing the fuel supply to the throat, engineers installed an additional butterfly valve at the top of the carburetor that restricts air flow. When you push the accelerator pedal to the floor and release it, the throttle linkage engages the choke linkage and closes the choke valves. At the same time, the throttle butterfly valve is held open to uncover the off-idle ports. Fuel enters the throat through the idle and off-idle ports and provides an extra rich starting mixture. A thermostat opens the choke valves slowly as the engine warms up and demands less fuel relative to the air flow. The thermostat ensures a smooth transition between cold and hot running requirements.

IGNITION SYSTEM

Two circuits make up your car's ignition system, and together they provide the voltage to run the starter and create the spark that ignites the fuel/air mixture in the combustion chamber. The primary circuit includes the battery, starter motor, alternator, ammeter or indicator light, the ignition switch, the ignition bypass wire, the ballast resistor, ignition coil, breaker points, and the condenser. The secondary circuit includes the ignition coil, the high voltage coil wire, distributor cap, distributor rotor, the spark plug wires, and the spark plugs.

Turning the ignition switch to "start" completes a circuit from the battery through the start relay and switch to the starter motor solenoid. At the same time, it completes a circuit through the starter motor solenoid and the resistor bypass wire to the positive side of the ignition coil.

The ballast resistor is placed in the circuit between the battery, ignition switch, and the coil to reduce the voltage to the coil during normal operation. Reducing the voltage lowers the coil's operating temperature and adds to its service life. During cranking, however, it is necessary to bypass the resistor because of the voltage drain imposed by the starter motor. If the resistor were included in the circuit during cranking, the battery would not have sufficient voltage to overcome the resistor and satisfy the demands of the starter motor and the coil.

The ignition coil is a step-up transformer that increases the battery's relatively meager voltage to anywhere from 8000 to 15,000 volts. That much voltage is needed to jump the spark plug gap. Current enters the coil through the positive terminal. A wire connecting the coil's negative terminal to the breaker point assembly in the distributor completes the primary circuit to ground through the grounded distributor. As long as the breaker points remain closed, we have a complete circuit.

Fig. 9-14. Breaker point assembly. Finger is resting on the rubbing block.

While the points remain closed the coil builds up voltage. The period of time during which the points are closed is referred to as the "dwell," and the degree of distributor shaft rotation that occurs during that time is called the dwell angle. You change the dwell by increasing or decreasing the point gap. Increasing the gap decreases the dwell; decreasing the gap increases the dwell. The longer the points remain closed, smaller gap, the more voltage will build up in the coil.

The ignition points, or breaker points as they are usually called, open and close the primary circuit. One side of the points assembly is stationary, and the contact point is attached to an arm of the assembly backing plate. The other side pivots on a stud affixed to the backing plate. The contact point is attached to a spring loaded arm the tension of which keeps the points in contact. See Fig. 9-14.

A cam with 4, 6, or 8 lobes (one lobe for each cylinder) protrudes through the breaker plate and rotates with the distributor shaft. See Fig. 9-15. As the cam rotates, the lobes contact a phenolic rubbing block attached to the movable side of the points assembly and open or break the circuit. See Fig. 9-16. A condenser connected to the points and grounded to the distributor body reduces arcing at the points and increases their working life span.

For simplicity's sake, let's once again consider only cylinder number one. The starter motor rotates the crankshaft. The crankshaft moves piston number 1 up toward the combustion chamber to compress the fuel/air mixture. At the same time, the crankshaft rotates the camshaft via the timing chain and sprockets, and positions the cam lobes in a way that permits both intake and exhaust valves to close tightly. The camshaft rotates the distributor shaft, and at a point in the crankshaft rotation before the piston reaches top dead center, the points cam lobe on the distributor shaft contacts the rubbing block, opens the points, and breaks the primary circuit. See Fig. 9-17.

135

Fig. 9-15. Breaker cam.

Electricity always takes the least resistant path which has been, until now, the primary circuit through the points to ground. When the circuit to ground is broken, the large voltage build-up in the coil escapes through the high voltage coil wire to the distributor cap.

Fig. 9-16. Cam lobe engaging the phenolic rubbing block and about to open the points.

A rotor which is keyed to and rotates with the distributor shaft is electrically connected to the coil wire by a spring loaded carbon pin in the cap at the base of the coil wire terminal (see Fig. 9-18), and a metal plate atop the rotor. When the points open in our example, the rotor is pointing to the number one spark plug wire terminal in the distributor cap. The electrical surge enters the distributor cap through the coil wire and the spring loaded carbon pin, travels along the metal plate on the top of the rotor, and leaps the gap between the rotor and the plug wire terminal. See Fig. 9-19.

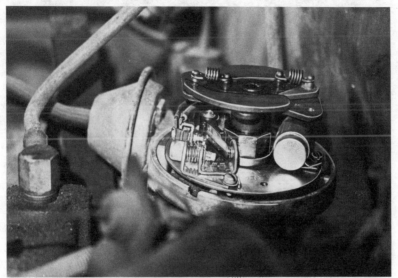

Fig. 9-17. Breaker points just opening to fire number one spark plug on the cylinder's compression stroke.

The electrical surge travels through the spark plug wire, the plug core, arcs across the electrode gap, and ignites the compressed fuel/air mixture in the cylinder. Only a fraction of a second elapses from the time the points open until the plug fires.

The engine is now idling at, let's say, 800 revolutions per minute, and each cylinder is firing at 10 degrees of crankshaft rotation before the piston reaches top dead center. What happens at higher engine speeds? Regardless of the engine's speed, the fuel/air mixture requires the same amount of time to burn. However, as engine speed increases, the piston passes through the compression stroke more quickly. If the plug continued to fire at the same time, a lot of the fuel/air mixture would be wasted.

In order to allow sufficient time for the fuel/air mixture to burn completely at higher engine speeds, engineers had to provide a

Fig. 9-18. Carbon pin in the center of the distributor cap, and the rotor contact plate.

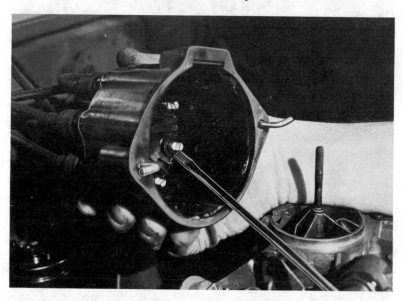

Fig. 9-19. Screwdriver points to plug-wire terminal inside the distributor cap.

Fig. 9-20. Centrifugal advance.

means for firing the spark plug sooner. This is called advancing the spark. During the automobile's design infancy, the driver advanced the spark by moving a lever on the steering wheel hub which acted through a linkage to move the magneto. Thankfully, these days the distributor advances the spark automatically.

CENTRIFUGAL ADVANCE

The centrifugal advance is a mechanical automatic advance unit that responds to engine speed. Generally speaking, this is how it works. A flyweight base plate is keyed to and rotates with the distributor shaft. The plate fits down into the distributor body (except for late model General Motors cars) and allows the top of the distributor shaft to poke through. The breaker cam fits over the distributor shaft and rests on the flyweight base plate. Two weights which pivot on posts attached to the base plate grip the base of the breaker cam assembly with hooked ends and permit the cam to rotate with the distributor shaft and the flyweight base plate. A pair of springs, one for each flyweight, keeps them tight against the base of the cam assembly. See Fig. 9-20.

As the engine speed increases so does the speed of the distributor shaft. Centrifugal force drives the flyweights out away from the shaft. As the flyweights pivot outwards, their hooked ends turn the breaker cam assembly in the direction of distributor shaft rotation and break the contacts earlier.

The centrifugal advance, however, reacts rather slowly to sudden demands on the engine. For example, opening the throttle suddenly at low engine speed would produce a terrible shudder from the engine until it catches up with the demand. In order to smooth out the transitions and make the car easier to drive, engineers designed the vacuum advance.

VACUUM ADVANCE

The distributor's vacuum advance responds to engine load, and it advances or retards the timing according to the amount of vacuum present in the intake tract. Most of these advance units take vacuum from a point in the carburetor throat just above the throttle butterfly valve. They provide no advance at idle, because pressure in the throat is high. Those units that do provide advance at idle take vacuum from the intake manifold where vacuum is high.

At steady throttle openings, intake tract vacuum is high. At modest high gear cruising speeds where engine speed is too low for the centrifugal advance to work, the vacuum advance unit provides the necessary advance. Vacuum applied to one side of the diaphragm and atmospheric pressure applied to the other work through a linkage to rotate the breaker plate in the opposite direction of the breaker cam rotation. See Fig. 9-21. This action

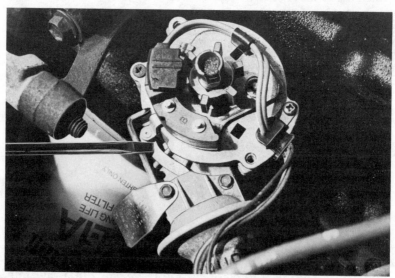

Fig. 9-21. Vacuum advance linkage.

brings the breaker cam lobe into contact with the points sooner.

If the driver makes a sudden demand on the engine such as pushing the accelerator pedal to the floor when the engine speed is low, vacuum in the intake tract is momentarily low. A spring in the advance unit moves the diaphragm, linkage, and the breaker plate in the same direction as the breaker cam rotation and causes the cam to engage the points later. It retards the timing and allows the other systems time to catch up to the driver's demands. The action smooths out the engine's response.

Fig. 9-22. Typical electronic distributor reluctor and pickup.

Most distributors reach full advance at an engine speed of about 3500 revolutions per minute. The vacuum advance works at the lower speeds, and the centrifugal advance takes care of the higher engine speeds. Modern distributors cannot reach full advance with only one of the advance units working.

ELECTRONIC IGNITION

The breakerless electronic ignition replaces the points and condenser with a magnetic pickup. A reluctor replaces the points cam. As a prong on the reluctor passes the magnetic pickup, the pickup sends an electrical signal to a control box where a transistor opens and closes the primary circuit. The transistor accomplishes the same job as the points in a conventional ignition. Because the reluctor never touches the pickup, no parts wear out. Once the system is adjusted, it should remain so. See Fig. 9-22.

The system generates more than twice the voltage of a points ignition, and it requires heavier gauge wires with thicker insulation. The rotor, distributor cap, coil, etc., perform essentially the same function as those in a points ignition. Longer spark plug life, the absence of periodic adjustments, and more efficient combustion offer real advantages over the breaker-point ignition.

CHAPTER 10

Engine Tune-Up

If you asked 100 drivers what "tune-up" means to them, you stand a good chance of getting 100 different answers. For some drivers, changing the spark plugs is enough, whereas others aren't satisfied unless a variety of parts are replaced and all of the appropriate adjustments made. From a professional's point of view, a tune-up is a series of procedures that restores the engine to the highest level of performance possible within the limits of the manufacturer's specifications.

Before the seventies when federal government standards for exhaust emissions became more and more severe, a tune-up was a reasonably simple process that an experienced mechanic could do almost by ear and feel. He could tune for the best performance within the confines of the design and quality of the components. These days, however, the mechanic has to conform to rigid rules, and any variation from the norm must be accompanied by an exhaust gas analysis. The mechanic is tuning for low emissions instead of high performance. You cannot ignore the emission controls. They are an integral part of the fuel, ignition, and breathing systems, and they are part of the tune-up.

A word of caution: aside from replacing a few emission control parts which we will discuss later, you should not remove, alter, or disconnect any part of the engine's emission controls. Under no circumstances should you deviate from the auto maker's recommendations for ignition timing or carburetor settings on an emission controlled engine unless the deviation is directed by the factory.

A word about replacement parts. Stay with the manufacturer's genuine replacement parts or with the quality brand names such as Delco, Autolite, MoPar, MotorCraft, Bendix, Champion, AC, etc. You might have to pay a little more, but the longevity of these parts will more than make up for the higher price.

Periodic tune-ups add life to your car's engine, improve fuel economy and performance. You should tune or have someone tune your car's engine at regular intervals that, at least, correspond to the manufacturer's recommendations. You can, however, benefit from more or less frequent tune-ups if your driving habits do not fit the norm used by manufacturers to arrive at their prescribed maintenance schedule.

One tune-up a year, usually in the fall, will satisfy the average 12 to 15 thousand mile-a-year driver. If you drive 40 to 50 thousand miles a year and mostly on the highway, a tune-up every 20 thousand miles should suffice. If you drive most of your miles in heavy stop and go traffic, a tune-up every 10 thousand miles might be a better bet.

In the absence of a schedule, your engine will tell you when it's time for a tune-up; acceleration will become sluggish, fuel mileage will suffer, the engine might stall at traffic lights or hesitate when you need acceleration; or, the engine might misfire at a variety of throttle positions or develop flat spots in the cruising range.

Before you begin the tune-up, park your car on a level spot, select "Park" (automatic transmission) or neutral (standard transmission), and set the parking brake. Working in your garage even with the door open can be dangerous. Frequently wind direction and velocity, air temperature and humidity will prevent poisonous exhaust gases from escaping the garage. To be safe, make an exhaust extension that reaches at least 6 feet beyond the door opening. A discarded vacuum cleaner hose works beautifully.

Select the tools that you will need and arrange them on the bench. You will need:

1. Combination wrenches
2. 8 and 12 inch straight bladed screwdrivers
3. Pliers
4. Ratchet, spark plug socket, socket set, 3, 6, and 12 inch extensions, swivel joint
5. Ignition wrench set
6. Ignition points gap and spark plug gap feeler gauges
7. Compression gauge
8. Dwell meter
9. Timing light
10. Volt-ohm-milliampere meter
11. Allen wrench set
12. Hand cloths

13. Fender cover
14. Masking tape
15. Oil can
16. Wire brush
17. Chalk
18. Breaker cam lubricant
19. Length of jumper wire with alligator clip on each end

Plug in your drop light and hang it from a convenient spot on the open hood. Read the instructions through carefully, then begin the tune-up.

COMPRESSION TEST

It's a good idea before you tune a high mileage engine to test for compression pressure. A compression test indicates the condition of the valves, piston rings, and head gasket. All of these components work together to seal the fuel/air mixture into the combustion chamber during the compression stroke. Compression leaks lead to inefficient burning of the mixture, and no amount of tuning will help the problem.

Start the engine and run it until it reaches normal operating temperature. Disconnect and plug all of the vacuum hoses associated with the air cleaner assembly. Label them with your own code. Locate, disconnect, plug, and label the distributor vacuum hose(s). See Fig. 10-1. Remove the air cleaner.

Remove the spark plug wires. Take hold of them by the plug boots, as shown in Fig. 10-2. Careful, it's hot around those plugs. Twist the boots back and forth and pull toward you. Never pull by the wires. As you remove the wires, label each one with the number that corresponds to the cylinder's number. See diagram in Fig. 10-3.

With your ratchet, appropriate length extension, and spark plug socket, loosen each plug as shown in Fig. 10-4. After you have loosened each plug, remove the ratchet from the extension and socket, and finish unscrewing the plugs by hand. A rubber bushing in the top of the plug socket will hold the plug into the socket. If you plan to reuse the spark plugs, handle them carefully. Dropping them or generally banging them around might crack the insulation and ruin the plug.

Ground the ignition system. Remove the high tension lead from the center of the distributor cap. Inside the rubber boot you will see the metal terminal on the end of the wire. Attach your jumper wire to that as shown in Fig. 10-5, and attach the other end of the jumper wire to a convenient nut or bolt on the engine.

Fig. 10-1. Remove all vacuum lines (PCV, distributor advance, etc.).
and plug source of vacuum.

Screw your compression gauge into spark plug hole number
one as shown in Fig. 10-6. Make sure that the rubber sealing
washer is in place. Top quality compression gauges come with a
variety of hose adapters to match the different plug hole threads

Fig. 10-2. Removing the high tension lead from the spark plug.

IN-LINE ENGINES:

Front	Front
1	1
2	2
3	3
4	4
	5
	6

CHRYSLER, AMERICAN MOTORS, and most GENERAL MOTORS V8 and V6 ENGINES:

Front		Front	
1	2	1	2
3	4	3	4
5	6	5	6
7	8	Left	Right
Left	Right		

FORD MOTOR CO. V8 and V6 ENGINES:

Front		Front	
5	1	4	1
6	2	5	2
7	3	6	3
8	4	Left	Right
Left	Right		

Fig. 10-3. Cylinder numbers and location.

that a mechanic is likely to encounter. Ford uses 18 millimeter course thread, whereas General Motors, Chrysler, and American Motors use a finer 14 millimeter thread. Some General Motors engines use a fine 12 millimeter thread. If you are using a rubber tipped gauge that you have to hold into the hole to effect a seal, you needn't concern yourself with adapter thread sizes.

Have an assistant get into the car, depress the accelerator pedal to the floor, hold it there, and crank the engine with the ignition switch. Stop cranking when the gauge needle reaches its highest reading. Jot the reading down on a note pad and go to the next cylinder.

Fig. 10-4. Removing a spark plug.

Compression values don't mean much without the manufacturer's specifications for new engines and the service limit. The compression values are listed in the factory service manuals used by dealer service departments. If you call or stop into your local dealer and ask graciously, he will probably look up the figures for you. Usually, you will find compression pressure be-

Fig. 10-5. Grounding the ignition system.

tween 100 and 150 psi. If all of the compression values are above 100 psi, the important thing to consider is the variation among the cylinders. It shouldn't exceed 20 to 40 psi.

If, for example, your Pinto reads 130, 140, 135, 145 psi, the engine is in good shape, and the compression values are within variation limits. If, however, cylinder number 2 returned a reading of 100, then you should expect some trouble. In order to determine if the piston rings, valves, or head gasket are responsible for the low reading, shoot several squirts of engine

Fig. 10-6. The compression gauge connection.

oil into the plug hole, and test again. If the reading improves, the rings haven't been sealing well. If the reading remains low, heavy carbon deposits aren't letting the valves close completely, or one of the valves is burned, or the head gasket is leaking. A head gasket will let coolant into the cylinder, and great clouds of white vapor will exit the exhaust pipe. Consult a professional mechanic. You will need a valve job, new rings, or a new head gasket.

TUNE-UP PARTS

Assuming that your compression test returned acceptable readings, you can begin the tune-up. You will need some or all of the following parts.

1. Spark plugs. In order to get the most from the ignition system, you should replace the spark plugs at each tune-up. If you insist on reusing them, brush the carbon deposits away from the electrode with a wire brush.
2. Ignition breaker-points assembly and condenser. Replacing the condenser is usually a preventative measure. When condensers fail, they do so completely, and a severe engine misfire results.
3. Fuel filter.
4. Air filter.

5. Positive crankcase ventilation valve (PCV valve).
6. Crankcase filter.
7. Distributor cap. Many professional mechanics routinely replace the cap as a preventative measure.
8. Rotor.
9. Ignition wires. A resistance test will determine the need for new wires.
10. Charcoal canister or filter as required.

You might not need all of these parts at every tune-up, but it is a good idea to have them on hand before you begin the tune-up. Any parts that you don't use for one tune-up will be available for the next one. When you buy tune-up parts for your car, state the year, make, model, engine type (in-line 4 or 6 cylinder; V8 or V6) and the engine size or cubic inch displacement. Usually, you will find the displacement on a decal atop the air cleaner. It will read something like this: 350 CID.

SPARK PLUGS

Remove the new spark plugs from their boxes and gap them. Electrode gap is measured in thousandths of an inch, and it will vary from .035 for older breaker point ignitions, to .080 for late model electronic, breakerless ignitions. You will find spark plug gap information printed on a decal or sheet metal panel in the engine compartment. See Fig. 10-7. The library is another source

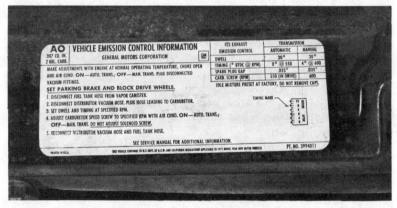

Fig. 10-7. Engine compartment tune-up information decal.

of information. They will probably have a copy of a professional mechanic's reference book such as Chilton's Auto Repair Manual 1979. These books are updated every year and contain tune-up specifications for all popular domestic cars.

Fig. 10-8. Measuring the spark plug electrode gap.

Measure the gap as shown in Fig. 10-8. Friction resistance will be moderate. Open or close the gap accordingly, as shown in Fig. 10-9. After you have gapped the plugs, set them aside in a safe place, and go on to the next step.

Wipe the plug wires clean with a cloth and examine the insulation for cracks, burns, or cuts. Pull back the spark plug boot and examine the metal terminal for greenish corrosion and greasy dirt buildup. Clean and polish the terminals with #600 sandpaper and breaker point contact cleaner.

PLUG WIRE RESISTANCE TEST

Beginning with plug wire number one (these should have been labeled for the compression test in Fig. 3-5) remove each wire from the distributor cap. Twist and pull up by the boot. After you remove wire number one, tear off a piece of masking tape, place it on the distributor, and write the number on the tape. Label each distributor socket immediately after removing the wire from it. Clean away any corrosion that you might find on the distributor end terminal.

Place your volt-ohm-milliampere meter on the fender. Plug the black meter test lead into the terminal marked "Comm," "Neg," or −. Plug the red meter lead into the terminal marked

Fig. 10-9. Adjusting gap. Bend side electrode up or down as needed.

+, V-Ohm-A. Turn the function dial to R×1, touch the ends of the test probes together, and zero the meter with the ohms adjusting knob. Turn the function dial to R×1000 or 1K. Touch one lead to one end of the plug wire and the other lead to the other end of the plug wire. See Fig. 10-10. You should get a reading of about 1000 ohms per inch of wire. A 20-inch wire will return a reading of about 20,000 ohms plus or minus 10%.

Significantly more resistance than prescribed indicates a deteriorating wire core. The plug wire core may be made from

Fig. 10-10. Testing plug-wire resistance.

carbon fiber which reduces static in fm radios, or it may be steel strands twisted together and used with resistance plug caps and resistance plugs to reduce radio static. If you have to replace a length of plug wire, make sure you use the type that came with your car.

Spark plug wire is sold from bulk rolls, and it is priced by the foot. Wire terminals for both the plug and the distributor ends are sold separately. Even though plug wires last a long time, it's a good idea to keep a length of it and some terminals on hand for future needs. If your test revealed a faulty plug wire, cut a piece from your stock to the exact length of the old wire. Install the new terminals as shown in Fig. 10-11 and place the wire back into its routing clips.

Fig. 10-11. Installing a new terminal, distributor end.

THE DISTRIBUTOR

Remove and service the distributor cap. In order to remove the cap from General Motors and American Motors V8 and V6 distributors, insert your screwdriver blade into the slot of the spring loaded cap screw as shown in Fig. 10-12. Press down and turn one-quarter turn in either direction to release the screw. You will have to completely remove the cap screws from some American Motors engines and from General Motors in-line 4 and 6 cylinder distributors by turning the screw counterclockwise. The distributor caps on all other makers' engines are held in place by one spring clip on either side of the cap. Insert a screwdriver as shown in Fig. 10-13 and pry the clip away from the cap.

Wipe the distributor cap clean. Examine the plug and coil wire sockets for corrosion. Look for cracks in the plastic, especially around the plug wire terminal towers. Examine the rotor electrodes in the cap (Fig. 10-14) for arcing corrosion. Make sure that the spring loaded rotor contact pin in the center of the cap moves freely. You can clean corrosion from the plug wire sockets and electrodes with #600 sandpaper and contact cleaner. If you tune your car every 10 to 12 thousand miles, you might want to replace the distributor cap every other tune-up. Tune-ups at 15 to 20 thousand miles should include a new cap.

INSTALLING A NEW DISTRIBUTOR CAP

Find the locating lug on the inside of the distributor cap, as shown in Fig. 10-15. Place the cap on the bench with the lug facing you. Find the same lug on the new cap and place it next to the old one with the lug facing you. Transfer the numbered pieces of masking tape to the plug wire terminals. Set the cap aside.

REMOVING THE ROTOR

The large diameter, noise suppression rotors are usually held in place by a pair of screws. Remove these as shown in Fig. 10-16. Note the locating dowels on the underside of the cap. These

Fig. 10-12. Removing the distributor cap from a General Motors V8 distributor.

fit into corresponding holes in the automatic advance unit. When you install a new rotor, make sure that these dowels line up with the correct holes.

Other rotors merely press on and pull off. These are located by a flat on the shaft that corresponds to a flat in the rotor (see Fig. 10-17), or it may be located by a slot or keyway in the distributor shaft and a corresponding lug in the rotor. Line these up when you install a new rotor. Remove the old rotor and discard it.

Fig. 10-13. Removing the cap from other type of distributor.

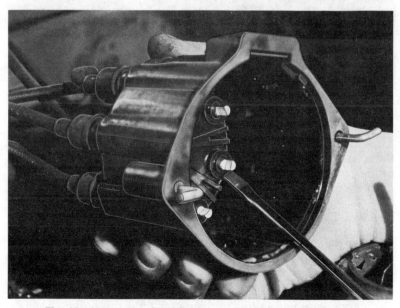

Fig. 10-14. Note the deposits on terminal electrode caused by the arc between rotor and electrode.

REMOVING AND REPLACING
THE POINTS AND CONDENSER

Make sure that the ignition is turned off. Disconnect the ignition coil primary wire from the points spring, as shown in Fig.
10-18. In some General Motors distributors, the primary wire is
secured to the points with the return spring tension. Release
the tension with a screwdriver and pull the terminal lug up. Remove the condenser wire.

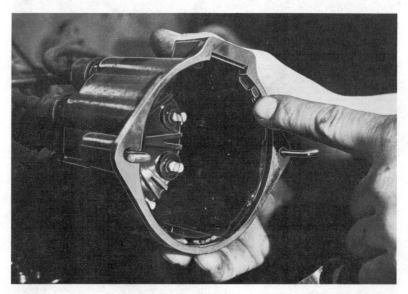

Fig. 10-15. Distributor cap locating lug.

Locate the points assembly mounting screw(s) and remove
them, as shown in Fig. 10-19. In order to avoid losing them to the
insides of the distributor, use a magnetic screwdriver. You can
magnetize any screwdriver by rubbing a magnet in one direction
along the length of the shaft. Locate the condenser mounting
screw and remove it as shown in Fig. 10-20. Lift the points assembly and the condenser out of the distributor.

Wipe the breaker cam with a clean cloth. Apply a dab of
breaker cam lubricant to your forefinger, rub it against your
thumb, and spread a thin layer of grease onto the breaker cam
as shown in Fig. 10-21. Always use special breaker cam lubricant.
Ordinary grease will liquify and splatter onto the points. Breaker
cam grease is available in most auto parts stores. It's a good

Fig. 10-16. Removing the rotor from a General Motors V8 distributor.

idea to install a new cam wiper as shown in Fig. 10-22. Do not lubricate the wiper. Install your new points and condenser by reversing the disassembly procedure.

Fig. 10-17. Rotor locating lugs.

ADJUSTING AND ALIGNING THE POINTS

Before you install the points assembly, make sure that the movable and fixed points meet squarely as shown in Fig. 10-23. If they don't, grip the fixed point brace below the point with your needle-nose pliers and bend it a little. Do not grip the contact with the pliers.

Fig. 10-18. Disconnecting the coil primary wire from the points.

You have to adjust the point gap when the points rubbing block is resting on the highest part of the breaker cam lobe. See Fig. 10-24. At this point the points are open widest. Turn the engine over by rotating the fan clockwise, or counterclockwise as seen from the front of the car. In order to determine which direction of engine rotation is normal for your engine, ask an assistant to crank it over while you watch which direction the fan and pulleys rotate. Note the distributor shaft rotation; it will save you time later. Stop turning when one of the cam lobes opens the points all the way.

Refer to the specification panel in the engine compartment for the correct point gap. Let's assume that it's .019. Select the appropriate feeler gauge and insert it between the contact points, as shown in Fig. 10-25. Loosen the points assembly lock screws a half turn or so. You want the assembly free enough to move

Fig. 10-19. Removing the points assembly mounting screws.

but not really loose, because the adjustments that you make are usually very small. Insert your screwdriver blade into the pry slot as shown in Fig. 10-26 and open or close the gap as necessary.

Fig. 10-20. Removing the condenser mounting screw.

Fig. 10-21. Lubricating the breaker cam.

Fig. 10-22. Installing a new cam wiper.

Fig. 10-23. Points meet squarely.

Fig. 10-24. Points rubbing block is on the highest part of the breaker cam lobe.

If the feeler gauge wobbles between the contacts without disturbing the movable arm, the adjustment is too loose. Remove the feeler gauge and reinsert it. If when you reinsert the feeler gauge the movable arm opens a little to admit it, you have ad-

Fig. 10-25. Measuring the point gap.

justed the gap too tightly. Friction drag on the feeler gauge should be light. Tighten the lock screws and measure the gap again. Sometimes tightening the screws will open or close the gap slightly.

You can adjust the point gap on some General Motors and American Motors V8 engine distributors by turning a spring loaded Allen cap screw, as shown in Fig. 10-27. The points assembly is not secured with a lock screw.

Turn the engine over by rotating the cooling fan counterclockwise or clockwise and look for the timing marks on the crankshaft pulley. Wipe the area clean. Next, locate the timing pointer

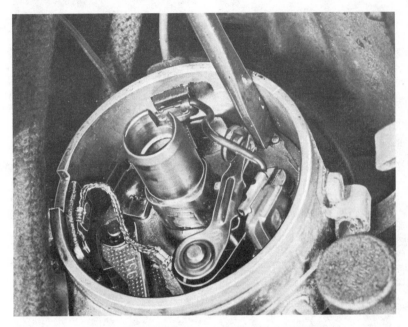

Fig. 10-26. Measuring the gap—most distributors.

in the engine casting. See Fig. 10-28. Wipe the pointer clean and lighten it with your chalk. Most modern crankshaft pulleys are marked in degrees of crankshaft rotation before and after top dead center with 0 indicating TDC. Find the timing figure for your car's engine and mark that line with chalk. The lightened lines will be easier to see under the timing light.

DWELL

Presumably, if you have correctly and accurately set the point gap, the dwell will be correct as well. Dwell is simply the number of degrees of distributor shaft rotation that the points remain

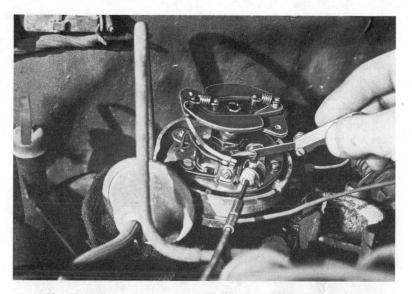

Fig. 10-27. Adjusting the gap on General Motors V8 distributor.

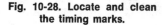

Fig. 10-28. Locate and clean the timing marks.

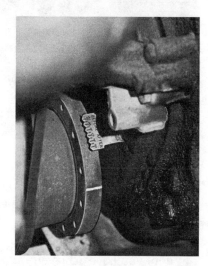

closed. You measure the dwell with a tach-dwell meter while the engine is running or cranking.

If you are working on a General Motors or American Motors car that has the spring loaded Allen cap screw points gap adjuster discussed earlier, make sure that the condenser and coil primary wire are properly connected to the points. Install the new rotor and distributor cap. Plug the high tension coil lead into the center of the distributor cap. Make sure that all plug wires are in the

163

proper sockets and that the boots are in place. Install the new spark plugs. Put a drop of engine oil on the threads and screw the plugs in by hand until the sealing washer seats. With your socket ratchet and plug socket, tighten the spark plugs one half to three quarters of a turn more. Connect all of the plug wires.

Locate the dwell adjusting window in the distributor cap. See Fig. 10-29. Place the tach-dwell meter in a convenient spot along the fender. Connect the leads and set the meter according to the maker's instructions. Start the engine and run it until the top of

Fig. 10-29. Dwell adjusting window.

the radiator is hot. You will find the correct dwell for your car listed on the information panel in the engine compartment. Read the dwell meter and compare the reading with the figure listed on the information panel. With the proper Allen wrench, reach into the adjustment window and turn the Allen cap screw in or out until you have achieved the correct dwell reading. Be careful to not get your hand caught in the fan blade if the distributor is mounted up front on the engine. Shut the engine off and close the adjustment window.

Most other cars don't provide a dwell adjustment window in the distributor cap. You can gap the points with a feeler gauge, install the rotor, cap, and spark plugs, start the engine, and check the dwell. About half of the time, you will be right. If you are not, you have to start over again.

There is, however, an easier way. Leave the distributor cap and rotor off and the spark plugs out. Hook up your tach-dwell meter. Disconnect the coil wire from the center of the distributor cap and attach it to ground as described in the compression test. Loosen the points assembly lock screws just enough so that you can move the assembly with a screwdriver in the pry slot. Place the dwell meter where you can read it quickly and accurately.

Have an assistant crank the engine with the ignition switch. Read the dwell and adjust accordingly. You should perform this procedure as quickly as possible to avoid overheating the starter motor. Tighten the points lock screws and test again. Tightening the screws might change the dwell by a degree or two. Readjust as necessary. Install the rotor, cap, spark plugs, and all wiring. Leave the tach-dwell meter connected. You are ready to time the ignition.

TIMING

Ignition timing sets the precise moment that the spark plug ignites the fuel/air mixture. It occurs at a specified number of degrees of crankshaft rotation before the piston reaches the top dead center (TDC) of its compression stroke, or in some cases, a few degrees after TDC. You can change the ignition timing by rotating the distributor assembly clockwise or counterclockwise while the engine is running. Timing specifications are stated in degrees before, at, or after top dead center at a specific number of engine revolutions per minute. The information will be printed on the information panel in the engine compartment. Use your tach-dwell meter according to the maker's instructions for counting engine revolutions.

Start the engine and let it run until the top of the radiator is hot. Shut the engine off and connect your timing light according to the manufacturer's instructions. Refer to Fig. 10-3 for the location of plug wire number 1, or refer to your taped labels on the wires. Make sure that all of your timing light connections are secure and that none of the wiring will foul the fan or belts. See Fig. 10-30.

Read the engine revolutions indicated on the tach-dwell meter and adjust to the correct idle speed for timing. Find the idle speed adjusting screw, as shown in Fig. 10-31. It will be located around the throttle linkage. Turn the screw clockwise to increase idle speed and counterclockwise to decrease idle speed.

Aim your timing light at the timing marks on the engine pulley and squeeze the trigger. Every time cylinder number one fires, the timing light will blink on and show you the timing marks and pointer in stop-action. Your chalked timing mark on the pulley

Fig. 10-30. Timing light connection.

should line up with the pointer. If the timing is incorrect, locate the distributor lock bolt, as shown in Fig. 10-32. Loosen it a few turns so that you can rotate the distributor by hand.

Fig. 10-31. Locate the curb idle adjusting screw.

If your distributor shaft rotates clockwise, turn the distributor assembly slightly counterclockwise to advance the timing and clockwise to retard the timing. Always make the adjustments in very small increments, and tighten the distributor lock bolt after each adjustment. Aim the light at the timing marks and check your adjustment. When you are satisfied that the timing is correct, disconnect the timing light, but leave the meter connected.

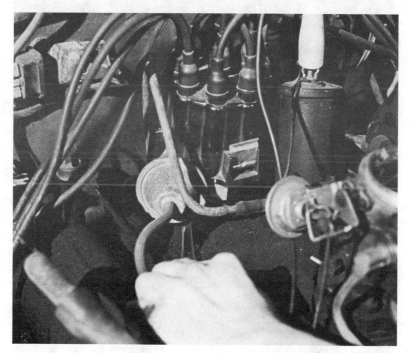

Fig. 10-32. Locate the distributor lock bolt and loosen it.

ADJUSTING THE CARBURETOR

Rough idling, poor gas mileage, stalling, hesitation, engine run-on, and a dirty exhaust are products of a badly adjusted carburetor. Late model, heavily emission controlled cars have plastic limiter caps installed over the mixture adjusting screws to maintain the factory settings. Under no circumstances should you attempt to adjust one of these carburetors beyond the curb idle adjustment. These carburetors have to be adjusted for low emissions with help from an exhaust gas analyzer.

Make all of your carburetor adjustments including curb idle after the engine has reached its normal operating temperature. See Fig. 10-31 for curb idle adjustment.

Fig. 10-33. Locate low speed mixture adjusting screw(s).

LOW SPEED MIXTURE ADJUSTMENT ON CARBURETORS WITHOUT LIMITER CAPS

Locate the mixture control screws as shown in Fig. 10-33. The carburetor may have one or two of these screws. With the engine idling and at operating temperature, turn the mixture screw clockwise until the engine speed, indicated by the tach-dwell meter, drops. Begin backing the screw out (counterclockwise) until the engine just reaches its smoothest and fastest idle speed. The procedure applies to both mixture screws. Adjust the curb idle accordingly. Disconnect the tach-dwell meter. Unplug and connect the distributor vacuum line(s).

AIR CLEANER

Many air cleaner assemblies contain two filters. The very large one cleans the air going into the carburetor, and the small one, located in the side of the cleaner body (Fig. 10-34), cleans the air going into the crankcase. In order to determine whether or not you need a new air cleaner element, place your drop light inside the element, as shown in Fig. 10-35. You should be able to see light through it from top to bottom all around the element. If you cannot, replace the filter. The crankcase filter should be re-

Fig. 10-34. New and old crankcase filter.

placed when the surface that faces in toward the carburetor throat becomes visibly dirty. It's a good idea to replace the crankcase filter at every or every other tune-up. Install the air cleaner, and connect all hoses.

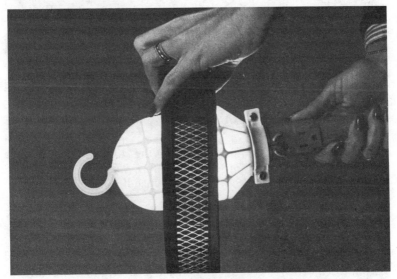

Fig. 10-35. Light should show through the entire surface of the filter element.

Fig. 10-36. Location of the fuel pump.

FUEL FILTERS

It is wise to routinely replace fuel filters at every tune-up. You will find these filters located in the carburetor float bowl just behind the fuel line at the inlet port, screwed to the outside of the float bowl, or in-line as a cartridge or canister filter. Locate the fuel pump as shown in Fig. 10-36 and trace the output line to the filter. The fuel pump should be on the driver's side on in-line 4 and 6 cylinder engines, and on the right side on V8 and V6 engines.

Carburetor Filter, In Bowl

Hold the large filter nut with a wrench and unscrew the fuel line nut with another wrench. Unscrew the filter nut and remove the filter. Note the position of any springs, washers, and gaskets. Note the position of the old filter and install the new one in the same position. See Fig. 10-37.

Outside the Bowl

Pinch the wire hose clamp together with a pliers and twist the fuel line off the filter. Use a clean cloth to absorb any spilled gasoline. Unscrew the filter and install a new one. The threads on the filter are tapered pipe threads, and the filter body should not bottom out against the carburetor. Screw the new filter in

Fig. 10-37. Remove fuel line from filter.

by hand until you can't turn it any more, then tighten it another turn with a wrench. Install the fuel line, start the engine, and check for leaks.

In-Line Filter, Cartridge

Pinch the hose clamps together with a pliers and slide them away from the filter. Twist the fuel line from each end of the filter and install the new filter. Make sure the flow indicator arrow points toward the carburetor.

In-Line Filter, Canister

These filters resemble small oil filters. Simply unscrew the canister from the top of the filter assembly, and install the new one in its place. Tighten only by hand and make sure that any sealing gaskets are in place. Start the engine and check for leaks.

CHECKING AND CLEANING THE CHOKE

Check the choke operation when the engine is cold. Remove the air cleaner assembly. Grasp the throttle linkage with your hand and open the throttle valve all the way. See Fig. 10-38. The choke valve should have closed. Ask an assistant to start the engine. Just after it starts, the choke should open about one-quarter of its travel. As the engine runs and warms up to operating temperature, the choke valve should gradually open all the way.

In many cases when the choke refuses to close, the linkage is binding or has become gummy. Spray the choke valve shaft and linkage with carburetor cleaner as shown in Fig. 10-39. After you have sprayed it, hold the throttle open and operate the choke by hand several times. Examine the linkage for loose pins or bent rods. Lubricate the external linkage with 10W motor oil or WD-40.

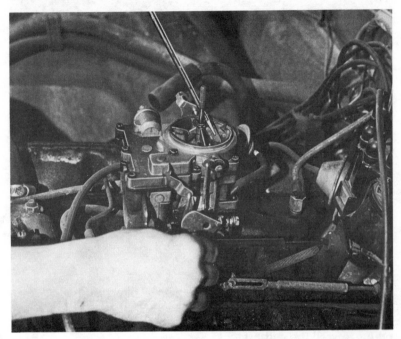

Fig. 10-38. Open the throttle by hand to close choke valve completely.

Clean and lubricate the throttle linkage and check all vacuum lines to see that they are properly connected and free from cracks or dry rot. Install the air cleaner assembly unless it interferes with servicing the PCV valve.

EMISSION CONTROLS

Engineers control exhaust emissions by altering engine design, changing calibrations, and by adding equipment to existing designs. Engine design changes include altering the bore and stroke dimensions to arrive at an ideal surface to volume ratio, changing the combustion chamber shape to create swirl patterns that lend themselves to more efficient burning, or adding a third valve

172

and a small chamber such as Honda's CVCC (controlled vortex combustion chamber) cylinder head.

A narrow bore and long stroke reduces the area of the combustion chamber for a given engine displacement. The smaller combustion chamber area decreases the amount of unburned gasoline left on the surface after combustion. Unburned gasoline leaving the exhaust is known as hydrocarbons. Lowering the compression ratio lowers combustion temperature and reduces the oxides of nitrogen in the exhaust.

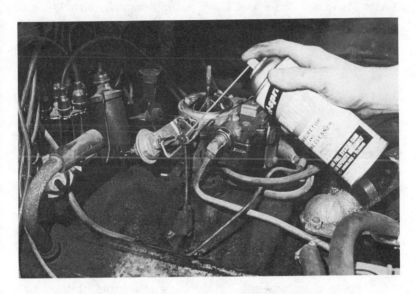

Fig. 10-39. Spray the choke valve and linkage with carburetor cleaner.

Calibrations include changes in ignition timing, fuel mixture, idle speed, and spark plug gap that produce more efficient combustion and reduce emissions. Mechanics can no longer adjust for best performance only. They have to compromise and achieve the best performance possible within the strict emission guidelines. In many cases, adjustments require sophisticated measuring and testing equipment.

Equipment added onto existing designs include exhaust gas recirculation devices, exhaust catalytic converters, positive crankcase ventilators, fuel tank and carburetor float bowl evaporation systems, and devices for controlling the temperature of the intake air supply. Some 1980 model Fords use a tiny engine compartment computer that electronically adjusts ignition and carburetor settings to compensate for driver demands and atmospheric conditions.

POSITIVE CRANKCASE VENTILATOR

The PCV valve began appearing on American cars during the early sixties. It controls the unburned gasoline or hydrocarbons that escape from the crankcase into the atmosphere.

During compression, a small amount of unburned gasoline blows by the piston rings and enters the crankcase. If allowed to remain, the gasoline would accumulate, dilute the oil, and reduce its effectiveness as a lubricant. Some form of ventilation system is needed to expel these harmful vapors. Years ago, air flow over a road draft tube open to the crankcase created enough vacuum to draw the vapors out. To complete the system, fresh air entered the crankcase through a vent located in the oil filler cap.

The PCV system uses engine vacuum to draw the vapors out of the crankcase. A hose attached to a vacuum port on the carburetor or intake manifold draws crankcase vapors from the valve cover or from a port cut into the crankcase casting. The vapors mix with the normal fuel/air mixture and are burned in the combustion chamber. Fresh air enters the crankcase through a vent in the oil filler cap.

The PCV valve allows air flow in only one direction. If a back-fire should occur in the manifold or carburetor, a check valve in the PCV will close and prevent a crankcase explosion. Because crankcase vapors are expelled into the atmosphere through the oil filler cap vent during full throttle, low engine vacuum, it is called an "open system."

The "closed system" makes a complete loop. Fresh air enters the crankcase through the air cleaner and a hose attached to a fresh air vent in the valve cover or in the oil filler cap. During periods of low engine vacuum, the vapors enter the combustion chamber through a filter in the air cleaner assembly. See crank-case filter, Fig. 10-34. The rest of the closed system works on the same principle as the open system.

A spring in the PCV valve moves a plunger against engine vacuum and permits less flow at high vacuum and more flow at low vacuum. The valve acts as a metering device, and it allows only as much of the vapor into the intake as it can handle.

TESTING THE PCV SYSTEM

Actually, you are testing for the presence of sufficient crank-case vacuum. Locate the fresh air entry. If it is a hose from the air cleaner to the valve cover as shown in Fig. 10-40, disconnect the hose from the air cleaner and plug it. If the fresh air enters the crankcase through the oil filler cap, simply remove the cap. Regardless of where the fresh air vent is, you will have to remove the oil filler cap to make the test.

Start the engine and allow about 30 seconds or so for the crankcase vacuum to build up. Hold a piece of ordinary stationery over the open oil filler hole and move it closer and closer until the vacuum draws it tight against the hole.

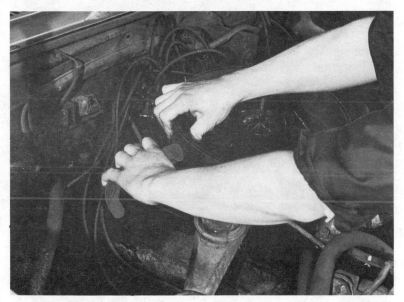

Fig. 10-40. Disconnect the crankcase fresh air hose from the air cleaner.

If the paper test shows no crankcase vacuum, remove the PCV valve as shown in Fig. 10-41. Start the engine and place your finger over the valve while the engine idles. You should feel full manifold vacuum. If you don't, remove the PCV from the hose and test again. If you experience vacuum now, you can assume that the valve is clogged. Install a new one.

Poor crankcase vacuum can be caused by air leaks around the oil sump gasket, the valve cover gasket, or any of the engine's many seals. Have a professional mechanic check it out for you. High mileage engines with badly worn piston rings will generate so much blow-by that the PCV system can't handle it. When this happens, you will see smoke coming from the oil filler cap while the engine is running. The only real cure is a new set of rings and the attendant machine work.

You should probably install a new PCV valve at every tune-up. Also, check the condition of the fresh air filter and all of the PCV hoses.

Fig. 10-41. Removing the PCV valve.

FUEL EVAPORATION SYSTEM

Fuel evaporation occurs at all times even when your car is sitting unused for days. Before emission control, the vapors from the gas tank and carburetor simply escaped into the atmosphere. Modern closed evaporation systems contain vapors in a charcoal canister when the engine isn't running. When you drive the car, engine vacuum draws the vapors into the combustion chamber where they are burned.

A liquid separator in the evaporation line near the gas tank prevents liquid gasoline from entering the canister. A filter cleans the fresh air as it enters the canister. Air enters the gas tank through a pressure vent in the gas cap, through a breather cap on the engine, or through a three way valve mounted near the tank. The vents allow air to enter the gas tank and replace the liquid volume. If the tank were not vented to the atmosphere, a vacuum would form and eventually collapse the tank. The carburetor float bowl is vented to the canister as well.

American Motors, General Motors, and Chrysler charcoal canisters have replaceable filters. These should be replaced at about every other tune-up or when they become noticeably dirty. The canister is usually located on the inner fender in the engine compartment, close to the radiator. Remove and label the vacuum

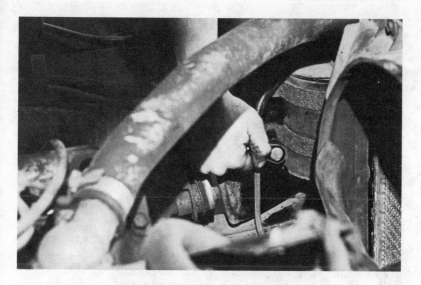

Fig. 10-42. Removing the charcoal canister from its bracket.

lines. Remove the canister from its bracket as shown in Fig. 10-42. Turn it upside down and remove the filter as shown in Fig. 10-43. Install the new filter. Careful, do not tear it. Replace the canister. Ford canisters do not have filters. The canisters on most models are located near the oil pan on the right side of the engine. You should install a new charcoal canister once every two years.

Fig. 10-43. Removing the canister filter.

INTAKE AIR TEMPERATURE CONTROL

Located in the air cleaner snorkel you will find a thermostatically or vacuum/heat sensor controlled air valve that determines whether the engine receives exhaust manifold heated air, or cool outside air. This valve is closed to outside air during engine warm-up. It permits only exhaust manifold heated air to enter the air cleaner which allows the engine to warm up faster. In winter when the air temperature is very low, the valve might never open, and the engine will receive only heated intake air. In the summer after the engine warms up, the thermostat or heat sensor and vacuum motor open the valve and admit cooler outside air to the carburetor.

In order to check the operation of the valve look into the air cleaner snorkel of a cold engine to see that the valve is closed. If it isn't, the linkage may be sticking. If it is closed, start the engine and watch to see that the valve opens as the engine reaches operating temperature. If it doesn't respond, the thermostat, vacuum motor, or heat sensor may be malfunctioning. Consult a professional mechanic.

Maintenance and adjustment of the remaining emission control devices must be left to a qualified and/or licensed mechanic.

Troubleshooting Chart

Symptom	Cause	Remedy
1. Engine won't turn over.	a. Faulty ignition switch. b. Loose or broken battery connections. c. Faulty neutral safety switch.	a. See a professional mechanic. b. Clean and/or tighten the terminals and/or clamps. Replace damaged cables. c. See a professional mechanic.
2. Engine won't turn over, starter motor clicks.	a. Insufficient battery voltage. b. Defective starter motor. c. Poor battery cable connections.	a. Charge the battery. b. See a professional mechanic. c. See 1(b).
3. Engine turns over but won't start.	a. Badly pitted or burned contact points. b. Defective condenser. c. Badly corroded distributor plug wire terminals. Eroded terminal electrodes. d. Moisture condensed inside the distributor cap, on the plug wires, inside the plug wire boots. e. Defective coil.	a. Install new points and condenser. Perform a tune-up. b. Install a new condenser. Perform a tune-up. c. Install a new distributor cap. d. Remove and dry the cap, dry the wires and boots, coat the wires, boots and distributor cap with a moisture repellent spray. e. Test the coil. Remove the large coil wire from the center of the distributor cap, hold it about ½ inch above a ground, crank the engine, and observe the spark. It should be a bright blue. An orange spark indicates a weak coil, no spark indicates a failed coil. Replace the coil.

	f. No fuel. g. Not enough gas at the carburetor.	f. Fill the tank. g. Clogged fuel filter. Install a new one. Faulty fuel pump. Have a professional test it. Replace the pump.
	h. Compression pressure too low.	h. Test to confirm. Consult a professional for the appropriate cure.
4. Hard starting, all conditions.	a. Weak spark caused by pitted points, failing coil, loose primary connections, shorting plug wires.	a. Examine condition of points, test coil, test plug wire resistance, check for loose primary circuit connections.
	b. Worn out or fouled spark plugs.	b. Replace or clean as necessary.
	c. Insufficient battery voltage.	c. Charge or replace battery.
	d. No gas at carburetor.	d. See 3(g).
5. Hard starting cold engine in all seasons.	a. Choke not working.	a. Check for binding linkage. Repair, clean, and lubricate as necessary.
	b. Carburetor flooding, vapor lock.	b. Fuel pump pressure too high, float valve not seating. Consult a professional.
	c. Very low compression.	c. Consult a professional.
	d. Low battery voltage, loose or corroded connections.	d. Check connections and clean or tighten as necessary. Test battery cells with a hydrometer. Charge or replace as necessary.
	e. In winter, too heavy an oil in the sump.	e. Change to a lighter weight oil.

Symptom	Cause	Remedy
6. Hard starting hot engine all seasons.	a. See category 4. b. Overheating engine.	b. Check coolant level. Drain and flush the cooling system, add fresh coolant. Check for leaks and clogged radiator fins.
7. Persistent engine stalling.	a. Worn out or fouled spark plugs. b. Idle too low. c. Badly pitted or corroded points. d. Choke stuck closed. e. Idle mixture too lean or too rich. f. Clogged PCV valve. g. Dirt or water in the fuel supply. h. Miscellaneous carburetor ills.	a. Clean or replace as necessary. b. Adjust idle speed. c. Replace and perform a tune-up. d. Clean and lubricate the linkage. e. Adjust or consult a professional for emission controlled cars. f. Replace valve. g. Have a professional clean the system. h. See a professional.
8. Steady misfiring at all engine speeds.	a. One or more defective spark plugs. b. One or more defective plug wires. c. Corroded or shorted distributor cap.	a. Remove the plugs and examine them. The bad plug will be black with carbon and wet with unburned gasoline. b. Perform a resistance test. Replace wires as necessary. Examine wire terminals and clean as necessary. c. Install a new cap.
9. Erratic miss at all engine speeds.	a. Dirt or water in the fuel system. b. Carburetor float level too high. c. Clogged fuel filter. d. Worn out or pitted points.	a. Have a professional clean the system. b. Have a professional reset it. c. Install a new filter. d. Install new points and perform a tune-up.

Problem	Cause	Remedy
	e. Defective condenser. f. Defective coil. g. Intermittent short in the primary circuit.	e. Install a new condenser and perform a tune-up. f. Test and replace coil. g. Have a professional check it for you.
10. Miss at high engine speeds only.	a. Worn out, incorrectly gapped, or fouled spark plug(s). b. Restricted fuel flow. c. Defective fuel pump. d. Carburetor high speed circuit dirty.	a. Replace, gap, or clean as necessary. b. Replace fuel filter. c. Replace pump. d. Have a professional overhaul the carburetor.
11. Engine miss at idle.	a. Improperly adjusted idle mixture. b. Restricted low speed circuit in the carburetor.	a. Adjust. b. Have a professional clean it.
12. Poor acceleration and high speed performance.	a. Retarded timing, pitted points, faulty condenser, worn spark plugs, faulty coil.	a. Perform a complete tune-up after testing the coil.
13. Poor fuel economy.	a. Leak in the fuel system. b. Faulty distributor advance. c. Poorly tuned engine.	a. Check for leaks and repair as necessary. b. Have a professional check it for you. c. Individual faults that contribute to poor fuel economy also indicate the need for a complete tune-up. Replacing worn plugs, for example, will help but not solve the problem.